FV

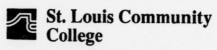

# Washington
## by Night

Photograph of medal on page 6 © Lee Anderson.
Photography copyright for pages 19–95 © Volkmar Wentzel
All other photography copyright as attributed.
All rights reserved
Copyright © 1992 Starwood Publishing, Inc.
All rights reserved.
No part of the contents of this book may be reproduced
without the written permission of the publisher.
ISBN 1-56373-019-7

Library of Congress Cataloging-in-Publication Data
Frank, Judith Waldrop, 1932–
    Washington by night/introduction by James M. Goode;
    foreword by Volkmar Kurt Wentzel; text by Judith Waldrop Frank;
    photographs by Volkmar Kurt Wentzel.

Includes bibliographical references
ISBN 1-56373-019-7
1. Washington (D.C.)—Pictorial works.   2. Washington (D.C.)—History.
I. Wentzel, Volkmar Kurt, 1915– / II. Title.
FI95.F78 1992
917.53404'4—dc20                     92-27670
                          CIP

# Washington by Night

Preface *by* VOLKMAR KURT WENTZEL

Introduction *by* JAMES GOODE

Captions *by* JUDITH WALDROP FRANK

Photographs *by* VOLKMAR KURT WENTZEL

STARWOOD PUBLISHING, INC.

Washington, D.C.

# Contents

# Photographer's Preface

## Silver Shadows

*by* VOLKMAR KURT WENTZEL

EARLY IN February of 1935 the Binghamton Press in upper New York State printed the following: "A 15,000-mile goodwill hike starting from Binghamton and going through North, Central and South America will be undertaken by two 19-year-old local boys, Volkmar Wentzel and William Buckley. Each will carry a knapsack filled with cooking utensils, blankets, a diary, a combination knife and hatchet and a camera to record the trip. Clothing will consist of a woolen shirt, riding britches and hightop leather boots as protection against snakes. They will interview President Roosevelt whom they have written . . . . "

After generally following the picturesque meanderings of the Susquehannah River, the last Washington-bound ride Bill and I had thumbed from Binghamton ended on the outskirts of Silver Spring, Maryland. From there it was a long, cold, and seemingly endless march down 16th Street straight to the White House.

President Roosevelt did not meet us at the gate. Not even a guard stopped us from walking right up the great portico with its big lantern swaying in the wind. We cupped our eyes for a peek through the glass door into the presidential mansion. No FDR.

With midnight upon us, we found shabby quarters two blocks away in the annex of the YMCA. A dim bulb dangled from the ceiling and tattered, peeling wallpaper cast eerie shadows around the room. Of the rickety cots lining each wall, two had been taken by sound snorers; judging from their gear, they might have been the last of the bonus marchers.

A frightened cry, "cockroaches!" startled me awake the next morning. Bill sat at the edge of his cot, red hair standing on end as he scraped such a monster off his boot. When I tried to calm him with the observation that more lethal creatures surely awaited us at the Isthmus of Tehuantepec, he got only more excited. Tehuantepec, I thought, would have a soothing, magic euphony like Tierra del Fuego, Katmandu, Pondicherry, and Rio de Janeiro; names that always made me want to see the world.

As we breakfasted in a grimy cafeteria on Pennsylvania Avenue, Bill simply could not get the roaches off his mind. Finally he declared, "I am going back. I am going home to my mother."

"But Bill," I countered again and again as we strolled aimlessly past the White House and along Pennsylvania Avenue, "We can't go back after all the things the Binghamton Press said we were going to do."

Bill was adamant. Nothing would change his mind. We split our joint fortune of one hundred forty dollars, money that we had raised laboriously with our newspaper routes and by selling our bicycles, my homemade kayak, and all our other boyhood artifacts. Quite suddenly, as Bill boarded a streetcar bound for Union Station, our teenage dreams came to an abrupt end.

Standing there alone, I was embarrassed to shoulder my big knapsack on which I had painted in large, red letters "New York to Rio." A sewer in front of a stately Victorian mansion at 18th and F Streets seemed the right place to dispatch this now humiliating burden. Little did I realize that I had picked the residence of Mrs. Robert Low Bacon, one of Washington's brilliant hostesses, and that one day I would be a guest at her charming black-tie dinners.

I was now on my own. Like many other people looking for a job and shelter in those Depression years, I queued up in the lobby of the *Washington Post* to thumb through the advertisements in free copies of the paper that were chained to a plywood lectern.

I was lucky, and found a tiny walk-up garret at 716 Jackson Place. In more splendid days it must have been a large closet or servant's quarters. From its dormer window I had a magnificent view of the White House and all of Lafayette Park. The once-elegant townhouse now harbored the law offices of "Tommy, the Cork" Corcoran, a very political New Dealer; Alberta Smith, the heavily rouged antique restorer and socialite; Simon Washington, our good caretaker; and Eric Menke, an eccentric architect and avid collector of books and maps who worked for the District Zoning Commission and the Municipal Architect's office.

Eric loved the city of Washington, and knew it very well. Through him I became aware that I now lived in what had been for a century the most historic residential area of the nation's capital. We became lifelong friends. His influence and a still-treasured copy of Brassaï's classic book *Paris de Nuit* that he gave me inspired the photographs in this book.

Around the corner and to the right of 716 Jackson Place, in what is now Blair House, the guest house of the Presidents, the Woodbury Blairs still lived. Woodbury was a fastidious gentleman of the old school. At precisely eleven o'clock every morning, with cane in hand, he rounded the corner at 17th Street for his martini and lunch at the Metropolitan Club.

At the other corner, in the Decatur House, I remember well the silverhaired Mrs. Truxton Beale. She was the last of a long line of distinguished Lafayette Square residents such as the Hays, Adamses, Dolly Madison, and Stephen Decatur. On hot Washington summer nights, long before air conditioning, I could see Mrs. Beale through a gossamer lace curtain cooling herself with a fan. I think of her as a living daguerreotype.

Behind Jackson Place, cobbled alleyways led to old carriage houses and stables. Simon Washington remembered the stories passed down to him that in the yard behind the Decatur House his slave ancestors had been auctioned off on the block. And in one of the coachmen's quarters partially converted to a photographic darkroom, I got to know Tom McAvoy, a Time Magazine photographer assigned to cover political Washington.

Most of Washington's White House photographer corps, who numbered about seventeen at the time, were then using the bulky 4" x 5" format Speed Graphics and Graflex cameras with Mendelsohn or Kalart flash guns. Only this equipment was considered professional, and generally, anything else was ridiculed and scoffed at.

In the face of this, Tom was one of the first to introduce the lively photo-reporting style that had evolved in Germany with the use of the miniature camera, faster optics, and improved films. The

Photograph by Clarence Jackson, WHNPA

dramatic Daumier-like photographs of the statesmen and celebrities of the Weimar Republic era taken by Dr. Erich Salomon, especially, had astonished the world.

Tom's great moment came when a flashbulb exploded close to FDR's face at a presidential dinner in the ballroom of the Mayflower Hotel. Flash was immediately forbidden near the president, and almost overnight the miniature camera revolutionized photoreporting. Looking over Tom's shoulder, I watched him print some of his first efforts taken with an early-model Leica.

I made up my mind then that photography would be my future. I applied for a job at the Underwood and Underwood Portrait Studios and News Agency at 1230 Connecticut Avenue. A brass plaque at the entrance reminded the visitor:

"These broad stairs have felt the firm tread of the President of the United States, Cabinet Officers and diplomats . . . the dainty steps of the world's social leaders . . . and the patter of little feet of happy children."

With some trepidation I climbed this grandiose, red-carpeted stairway for an interview with a Mr. Rubel. It was brief. He summarily decided that I would be a darkroom technician at $12.50 per week, and ordered Marcellus, a cheerful new co-worker, to conduct me down the backsteps to a grim, netherworldly sweatshop. My job was to mix big stoneware crocks full of hypo and developers for film and paper, and stir them with big wooden paddles badly frayed by the caustic brew. The chemicals had to be weighed separately on a rusty scale according to formulae thumbtacked to the wall. Not until after the Second World War would convenient ready-mixes become standard.

In addition, I learned to enlarge, contact-print, and gold-tone portraits. I loaded holders, developed film, and whenever needed went on sittings with the portrait photographers to carry and set up the heavy lights and 8" x 10" view cameras.

The sittings could be fascinating. We photographed Senators, Congressmen, diplomats, debutantes, and some charming (and not so charming) society ladies. Once, during hearings at the Senate

up the embassy drive. "Set your focus at twelve feet and stop down to five point six when she's on the landing, then for a close-up at the bottom, change to six feet and stop down to eleven, and, don't forget, turn your holder and pull the slide."

It all happened rather quickly. As the elegant, aristocratic Madame de Laboulaye descended the stairway, I got her proud and well poised on the landing. This picture made the Sunday Evening Star society rotogravure page. But the second negative was hopelessly overexposed because in the excitement I forgot to stop down. Luckily for me, Mr. Rubel liked the first shot and never having seen the second, he assigned me my own speed Graphic camera.

Office Building, in one of the corridors we collared the publicity-shy financier and banker, John Pierpont Morgan. We sat him down on a black fiber lighting case and before the poor man realized what was happening, we had taken his portrait.

During my time at Underwood and Underwood, I saw much of the inside of Washington, the offices on the Hill, and the splendid interiors of many embassies and private residences. Some, sadly, no longer exist. I also learned a lot, but what fascinated me most were the three photographers in the news department. Whenever they "souped" (developed) their film, I overheard exciting stories about visiting dignitaries and the latest scoop around town. I longed to be one of them.

One day, quite unexpectedly, I got my chance when one of my heroes and also one of the first White House photographers, Clarence Jackson, asked me to come along to the French Embassy to get some shots of Madame de Laboulaye, the wife of the ambassador.

Clarence, with his hat and press card tucked in the band, reminded me of both Humphrey Bogart and "Weegee," the famous New York city street photographer of the time. Jackson chain smoked, carried a hip flask, and exhaled a breath that could be smelled a yard away. He was superstitious, and would never fold his Graphic for fear that it would get out of synchronization and focus. Yet, with a mix of compassion and cool detachment he had an eye for drama and an instinct for the human element in pictures.

"We'll get her coming down the steps," he told me as we walked

second, he assigned me my own speed Graphic camera.

Back in the Underwood dungeon, our negatives were developed quickly, fixed, barely washed, and enlarged while still wet. With the wirephoto not yet in use at Underwood and Underwood, a dozen 8" x 10" glossy prints had to be made of every news event for the five local Washington papers and for others across the country. Speed was of the essence, otherwise the emulsion melted in the enlarger, often with bizarre results that might qualify as photographic art today. Sometimes we had to send our prints to distant cities by distinguished-looking Pullman porters, who were tipped two dollars on this end and two at the other end.

I was so proud of my newly assigned Graphic that I used every spare moment for practice. With the camera and a Crown tripod slung over my shoulder and Brassaï's images of Paris in mind, I explored Washington's grand avenues, plazas, and carefully-planned vistas. My range was limited only by the size of the holes I could patch in the soles of my shoes.

I was enchanted by the ethereal images revealed by the witchery of night. Floodlights etched familiar landmarks against the velvet sky. The Capitol, the Washington Monument, and the Lincoln Memorial glowed as if from within. I made many pictures in the heavy atmosphere of damp and foggy nights, when diffused light reduces scenes to their simplest elements.

Sometimes, during the time exposures, I highlighted distinctive outlines with the flashbulbs popular at the time. Focusing was done on the groundglass under the cover of a black cloth. The image was upside-down, of course, and often I had to use a flashlight to compose the framing of the picture.

Like a latter-day Eugene Atget, I always used a tripod. My trial-and-error exposures ranged anywhere from seconds to several minutes. If, after developing my film, I felt that the composition or exposure could be improved, I often returned to my subjects the same night. Washington streets were perfectly safe then. In my lonely quest I could go anywhere I pleased. Sometimes I photographed until the birds began to sing and the sun rose over the dome of the Capitol.

At the Lincoln Memorial I bribed the night watchman with prints of previous efforts to switch on the banks of light above for more dramatic effects. The infinite beauty and the refractions of light, I discovered, could create the mysterious moods and drama that make a great difference in the final print.

The amber twilight of the darkroom and the alchemy of a print coming alive in the gently rocking developing tray is a childhood memory vivid to this day. I must have been about nine years old when my father and I built a camera obscura, the forerunner of all cameras, with a principle known to Aristotle. Using a pinhole instead of a lens, we tested our dark chamber in a royal park near our house in Dresden, Germany. Our first picture was the marble statue of a voluptuous Medusa with snakes as hair and a muscular Hercules wrestling a writhing python.

I was fortunate that my father was a distinguished chemist and one of the best authorities on the subject of photographic emulsions. While pursuing his doctorate he had studied under such brilliant photographic pioneers as Prof. Dr. Herman Vogel, the discoverer of panchromatic sensitization, and Prof. Dr. Adolf Miethe, a renowned designer of lenses, pioneer in color photography, and teacher at the Technische Hochschule in Berlin.

For our pinhole pictures we mixed our own light-sensitive emulsion of gelatin and silver halides that we, or rather my father, coated with great dexterity on 9 x 12 cm glassplates.

"When we expose these plates to the image projected in the camera," my father explained, "the microscopic, light-sensitive silver halide crystals embedded in the transparent gelatin trap the tracery of light as a latent image. You can't see it, but when immersed in the developer this image is converted by chemical action to a very thin layer of metallic silver, possibly as thin as the frosting breath on a window pane."

The Englishman Fox Talbot, one of the fathers of photography, described the phenomenon this way. "The most transitory of things, a shadow, the proverbial emblem of all that is fleeting and momentary, may be fettered by the spells of 'our natural magic' and may be fixed forever in the position which it seemed destined for a single instant to occupy."

My early exposure to the eloquence of the delicate gradations of the silver-gelatin "shadows," awakened my lifelong fascination with photography, professionally and personally.

I surreptitiously printed some of my night pictures on Underwood and Underwood's best portrait paper. These, happily, were awarded some golden prize stickers by the Royal Photographic Society of Great Britain, and more importantly, on January 2, 1937, landed me a job on the photographic staff of the National Geographic Society.

My night photographs had now become a passport to the world. The editors of the Geographic sent me on many fabulous assignments to all ends of the earth. On one of these, a journey that took me around the fringes of the entire Atlantic Ocean, my boyhood dreams were more than fulfilled. As the Pan American clipper banked around the Christ statue on Corcovado for a landing in Rio de Janeiro, I could not help but think of the knapsack that I had stuffed down Mrs. Robert Low Bacon's sewer.

Thanks to photography, I can look back upon a rich and rewarding life. The Washington negatives that I reprinted recently for this book became a time capsule that brought back happy memories.

Ansel Adams once said, "The negative is the equivalent to the composer's score—and the print is the equivalent to the performance." I would hope that with this performance the reader will share some of the beauty I have seen and the wonders that can be captured with photography's silvery shadows.

Photograph by Fred J. Maroon

# Introduction

## The Creation of Monumental Washington in the 1930s
### *by* JAMES GOODE

AS A YOUNG MAN of nineteen Volkmar Wentzel arrived in Washington from his home town of Binghamton, New York in the midst of the Depression in 1935. After landing his first job as a darkroom technician, Mr. Wentzel learned the art of photography and became absorbed with recording on film Washington's vast new public buildings, sculpture, and landmarks. He worked a day job and consequently took his remarkable photographs during the nighttime. After a distinguished career as a National Geographic Society photographer, Mr. Wentzel recently discovered and reprinted these images from old negatives while cataloging his personal photographic archives. The publication of Mr. Wentzel's thirty-nine outstanding black-and-white photographs of Washington architecture and sculpture taken in the 1930s provides a valuable perspective on the enormous changes then taking place in the nation's capital. My survey of the physical and economic growth of Washington then, complements Mr. Wentzel's and helps establish the historical context of his photographs. We are also fortunate in having Mrs. Randolph Frank write the lively captions for Mr. Wentzel's pictures. The three of us, friends for over a decade through our joint membership in the Literary Society of Washington, have worked as a team on this book.

### MONUMENTAL WASHINGTON

The monumental character of central Washington was mostly established in the 1930s with the enormous volume of construction by the federal government in the classical mode. During the decade more than sixty new government buildings, bridges, and highways were either completed or begun. This construction helped fulfill Pierre L'Enfant's dream of a national capital of dignity and grandeur.[1] The 1930s architecture complemented the important government buildings erected before the Civil War: the White House, U.S. Capitol, Treasury Department Building, Patent Office Building, and old Post Office Department Building at 7th and F Streets. All were built in the neoclassical style. Another surge of federal construction occurred

in the 1960s, especially in Southwest Washington and the suburbs. But these buildings, mostly built in the bland International Style and clad in concrete rather than marble or limestone, are not the ones that come to mind when one thinks of the remarkable aspects of Washington.

Little economic or social change occurred in Washington between the stock market crash of October 1929 and 1931. The federal government—the city's main business—continued to stabilize jobs and growth. By 1932, however, the effects of failed banks and lost fortunes had begun to erode the city's real estate market. The private construction boom of the 1920s had come to an abrupt halt when developers found they could no longer find banks to lend money. The collapse of the construction industry, the failure of dozens of businesses as well as four major Washington banks, and President Herbert Hoover's freezing of new federal jobs in the city all contributed to poor economic conditions. For Washington, the winter of 1932–1933 was the darkest of the decade as soup lines lengthened and unemployment soared. The economic crisis in Washington caused the greatest change for the lower and upper classes; it affected the middle class the least because most had relatively secure jobs with the federal government or worked for businesses that served federal workers. Few of the wealthy Washington families lived solely on speculative earnings so they did not feel the immediate effects of the crash. Blue-chip stocks, which initially continued to pay dividends, helped maintain their large houses during the first two years of the Depression. But by 1932, as economic conditions worsened, many of Washington's rich had to sell their great houses around Dupont Circle and along Massachusetts and New Hampshire Avenues. Their owners retired to smaller second homes elsewhere.

Not all of the rich lost their large houses, however. One example, photographed by Mr. Wentzel in the Depression was Decatur House, built by Commodore Stephen Decatur in 1818 on Lafayette Park. The physical appearance of this landmark has changed since Mr. Wentzel photographed it in 1936. His mystical nighttime photographs show not only the Victorian door and window hoods which General Edward Beale installed in the 1870s but the intriguing dilapidated rear wing facing H Street. The mansion assumed its present appearance when Mrs. Truxton Beale commissioned architectural historian Thomas Waterman to restore it to its original design in 1944 soon after architect Benjamin Latrobe's watercolor drawings of the house were discovered in a local antique shop. Mrs. Beale, the last resident here, bequeathed the mansion in 1956 to the National Trust for Historic Preservation, which maintains it today as an historic house museum.[2]

## "BONUS ARMY" AFFAIR

No mention of the Depression years in Washington would be complete without recalling the arrival and dispersal of the Bonus Army. Even though Mr. Wentzel did not photograph this event, its historical importance needs to be mentioned to show the gravity of the economic conditions of the nation in the early years of the decade. It was the most dramatic event to occur in the city during the 1930s. In May and June 1932, thousands of unemployed World War I veterans came to Washington. The group set up impromptu camps at various sites within the city. Under the provisions of a 1924 law bonuses were to be paid to the veterans in 1945. They hoped to pressure Congress into amending the law to provide for immediate payment. Many Congressmen felt intimidated by the hundreds of veterans camped out on the Capitol grounds; others saw them—unrealistically—as a Communist threat. The three District commissioners, who governed the city, also were hostile to the group.

Washington police chief Pelham Glassford, who had served as a brigadier general in the United States Army in Europe in World War I, was more sympathetic to the veterans, providing food as well as space for most of them in a makeshift camp along the banks of the Anacostia River. There they built huts from packing crates, scraps of lumber, and canvas. Chief Glassford's sympathy for the former soldiers cost him his job when the affair ended.

Buckling under administration pressure, Congress voted on June 15, 1932 to sustain the original law which did not provide payment of the bonus to the veterans until 1945.[3] Then Congress adjourned, leaving 10,000 homeless veterans stranded. When the Treasury Department insisted that the government remove those members of the "Bonus Army" camping in condemned and abandoned buildings within the Federal Triangle area so that long-planned demolition could proceed, the District commissioners took action. They moved the city police to the site. In the ensuing scuffle the police fired on the veterans, injuring several.

Shortly thereafter, on July 28th, President Hoover ordered General Douglas MacArthur to evict the veterans. Among the army officers assisting MacArthur were Major Dwight D. Eisenhower and Major George S. Patton. In a dramatic move, MacArthur rode on horseback at the head of the military forces that included six tanks with mounted machine guns and 600 infantry troops with drawn bayonets. After the soldiers fired tear gas to force the veterans to leave the abandoned Federal Triangle buildings near 4th Street, a few veterans pelted the soldiers with bricks. The troops opened fire, killing several veterans. That night, MacArthur marched to Anacostia and burned the makeshift camp. Although MacArthur dispersed the vast majority of the "Bonus Army," 3,000 returned to Washington after Roosevelt's inauguration, less than a year later. This time, the president allowed them to camp at Fort Hunt near Alexandria, and provided tents and food. Eleanor Roosevelt visited the veterans there a number of times to listen to their requests for work. The formation of the Civilian Conservation Corps, which provided jobs for half of the veterans, resulted from this second encampment. Congress finally voted to pay the two billion dollars in bonus pay to the veterans in 1936.[4] The harsh treatment of the Bonus Army by the Hoover administration aided Roosevelt in his presidential campaign and directly affected his New Deal program of finding jobs for millions of Americans out of work.

## BOOM CITY

The inauguration of Franklin D. Roosevelt in March 1933 served as a turning point for Washington's prosperity. Economic growth stemming from the New Deal spurred the construction in Washington of federal buildings, bridges, parkways, outdoor sculpture, and the creation of new parks. The enormous amount of legislation initiated by his administration and adopted by the Democratic Congress his first year in office resulted in dozens of new government bureaus designed to create jobs for Americans across the country. By 1935 the president had increased the number of civil servants in Washington by 40% to more than 100,000. The number increased to more than 160,000 federal workers by 1939. They swelled the city's population by 36%, from 487,000 to 663,000 by the end of the decade.[5] Indeed Washington quickly became the only boom city in the nation. Every sector in Washington showed growth. For example, car sales in Washington, at 23,000 in 1929, had dropped to 13,000 in 1932, rose to 18,000 in 1934, and soared to over 32,000 in 1935. By 1936, local department store sales as well as residential construction exceeded the prosperous record set in 1929.[6]

By mid-decade, while other major American cities suffered from economic decline, Washington experienced physical growth and enjoyed a high degree of intellectual excitement because of the many new social programs introduced by Roosevelt.[7] In surveying the Washington scene in 1936 journalist Oliver McKee, Jr. wrote: "Washington will remain a boom town as long as the New Deal remains, and for those who man the guns it will continue to offer not only good pay but thrills and romance aplenty, and life in the grand manner."[8] The presence of Roosevelt's advisors, known as the "brain trusters," who shaped New Deal policies, contributed to the sense of a new order and change. The New Deal programs regulated all phases of industry nationwide. The number of lobbyists who came to solicit government contracts doubled in number as did the number of press corps who arrived to cover the constantly breaking news in the capital.

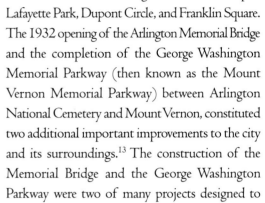

Prior to the New Deal, Washington had been seen as an appendage to New York City. That changed as Washington took its place beside New York as a power center with the creation of the many regulatory agencies established in the capital, including the newly formed Securities and Exchange Commission which regulated the New York stock market.[9]

To provide office space for its New Deal agencies, the federal government commandeered hotels, apartment houses, and even mansions. The great increase in the number of federal workers resulted in a Washington housing shortage and high real estate prices in the nation's capital by mid-decade.[10] Most workers felt they could endure these inconveniences in return for enjoying the excitement of living in a newer, more beautiful, and more powerful nation's capital.[11]

## CITY OF TREES

During the 1930s journalists described Washington as the most beautiful city in the country for its scores of new, white, classical government buildings and memorials; its expanded park system; and its streets lined with great trees. In such blocks as New Hampshire Avenue at Dupont Circle the great elms met overhead to create a glorious tunnel of green. Mr. Wentzel's dramatic photographs of the public sculpture in Dupont Circle and Scott Circle, surrounded by lush landscaping, reminds us that before World War II Washington was popularly known as "the city of trees." By the mid-1930s Washington's bureau of parks maintained 125,000 trees along city streets and planted an additional 4,000 trees annually.[12]

The government dramatically began to improve the core of the city in 1934. By clearing the Mall of the last vestiges of the Victorian park conceived and partly realized by Andrew Jackson

Downing in the 1850s, and grading and restoring it to the original design as envisioned by Pierre L'Enfant, the government created a great open greensward unbroken from the Capitol to the Lincoln Memorial.

The Park Service also repaired and cleaned the Washington Monument for the first time since its completion in the 1880s. Later in the decade the Park Service redesigned and relandscaped Lafayette Park, Dupont Circle, and Franklin Square. The 1932 opening of the Arlington Memorial Bridge and the completion of the George Washington Memorial Parkway (then known as the Mount Vernon Memorial Parkway) between Arlington National Cemetery and Mount Vernon, constituted two additional important improvements to the city and its surroundings.[13] The construction of the Memorial Bridge and the George Washington Parkway were two of many projects designed to celebrate the bicentennial of George Washington's birth in 1932.[14] Congress also funded the construction of Rock Creek Parkway in the Capper-Cramton Act in 1930. Washington was different from other cities in that the federal government planned, designed and paid for most of its parkways.[15] These new transportation arteries helped accelerate the movement of residents of the city to the suburbs where they could find less expensive housing. For the first time ever new residential construction in the Maryland and Virginia suburbs exceeded that in the city. By 1939 Arlington, Virginia was the fastest growing county in the nation.[16]

The city's park system continued to expand during the 1930s. In 1936 the National Park Service completed Meridian Hill Park at 16th and Euclid Streets. Influenced by Italian Renaissance landscape architecture, it was designed by Washington architect Horace Peaslee as the city's most elegant formal park and was built at a cost of $2.5 million.[17] Steps also were taken in 1932 to secure the 90-acre Theodore Roosevelt Island adjacent to Georgetown as a public park.[18] Another important addition to the city's park system came in 1935 when the government bought the entire length of the Chesapeake and Ohio Canal between Georgetown and the Maryland line.[19]

## SENATE PARK COMMISSION

The underpinning of the planning and classical style of the Federal Triangle and many other new government buildings in Washington in the 1930s lay in the work of the Senate Park Commission of 1901–1902. The Commission, created by Senator James McMillan, enlisted leading architects, landscape architects, and sculptors, including Daniel Burnham, Charles F. McKim, Frederick Law Olmsted, and Augustus Saint Gaudens, to recommend ways to physically improve the plan of the nation's capital. Many of their comprehensive plans—such as the opening of the Mall as a greensward—were carried out by President Franklin D. Roosevelt. During the early 20th century the "City Beautiful Movement," supported by civic leaders across the nation, pushed for such aesthetic urban improvements as new parks and major Beaux Arts public buildings. They made Washington, D.C. their model to follow.

The enormous growth of the federal government during and after World War I rendered insufficient the original three small locations proposed by the Senate Park Commission for office building construction by the federal government. The 30,000 government employees in the city in 1916 had doubled to 60,000 by 1926. Almost half of the government offices in Washington occupied rental buildings or temporary war structures, resulting in considerable inconvenience and expense. The Commerce Department was housed in over 20 different locations. Both the high rental costs and the inefficiency of having one bureau's offices widely scattered across the city caused Congress to take action. Congress passed the Public Buildings Act of 1926 designating the Federal Triangle site, then a blighted area including a large public market, industrial buildings, stores, and small office buildings, as the commodious new location for the massive complex.

The Federal Triangle was the most important government construction project of the 1930s in Washington. This group of eight buildings, designed in a unified fashion, bounded by 15th Street on the west, Pennsylvania Avenue on the north, and Constitution Avenue on the south, covers 70 acres. The Federal Triangle project, built between 1928 and 1937, solved the critical shortage of government office space in the nation's capital. Built midway between the Capitol and the White House, the complex of office buildings provided convenience and architectural harmony. Mr. Wentzel's nighttime photographs of the driveway and courtyard of the Labor Department Building as well as the south facade of the National Archives Building elegantly convey the grandeur of these structures.

The creation of the monumental Federal Triangle structures, designed to house 25,000 civil servants, bolstered the federal government's image of grandeur and permanence. In accordance with the Senate Park Commission plan, the design of the Federal Triangle complex would complement the classical style favored by Washington, Jefferson, and L'Enfant for the early government buildings. The classical style employed in the Federal Triangle buildings does not, however, conform to one architectural order. The Federal Triangle's architects based their designs on a variety of classical orders including the architecture of ancient Rome, the Italian Renaissance, and 18th-century France. Greater diversity and architectural interest was the result.[20]

## DESIGN OF THE FEDERAL TRIANGLE

The major influence on the design of the Federal Triangle was the concept of the Louvre-Tuileries complex.[21] The architects envisioned two great open ceremonial spaces based on Parisian design to unify the Federal Triangle project. They consisted of the Circular Plaza designed for the center of the complex on 12th Street, and the Great Plaza, terminating the western end of the Federal Triangle between the Post Office Department Building on 13th Street, and the Commerce Department Building on 14th Street. Two board members contributed to the design of these great spaces: William A. Delano for the Circular Plaza and Arthur Brown, Jr. for the Great Plaza.

While Presidents Calvin Coolidge and Herbert Hoover took initial interest in seeing the Federal Triangle completed as designed, the Depression-era administration of Franklin D. Roosevelt actually realized its basic completion. But Roosevelt never authorized the razing of the 1899 Romanesque Revival Post Office, needed to complete the Circular Plaza, nor razing the District Building, needed to complete the Great Plaza. These serious setbacks resulted in the use of the open space behind the District Building as a massive and unsightly outdoor parking lot for almost sixty years.

Working assiduously from 1927 to 1931 the Board of Architectural Consultants revised and perfected the skeletal plans of the Federal Triangle complex. They were strongly influenced by the Commission of Fine Arts, whose members favored the Senate Park Commission Plan of 1901–1902, as well as by several other government agencies, including the Public Buildings Commission, the National Capital Park and Planning Commission, the Office of the Supervising Architect of the Treasury, and the Washington Board of Trade.[22] Each member of the Board of Architectural Consultants—the six private architects and the Supervising Architect of the Treasury—contributed by designing specific buildings in the complex. All of these nationally prominent Beaux Arts architects, including John Russell Pope and William Bennett, worked skillfully as a team employing the classical mode. The only other office building construction project of this magnitude carried out in the United States during the 1930s was the building of Rockefeller Center in New York City.[23]

## ART AND SCULPTURE

During the design and construction process of the Federal Triangle architects worked closely with the sculptors to make certain that the more than 100 outdoor sculpted pediments, relief panels, bronze doors, and statues were in harmony with their buildings.[24] However, artists created murals and sculpture in the interiors of only three buildings: the Post Office Department, Justice Department, and the National Archives. More than eight dozen murals, painted by such renowned muralists as Henry Varnum Poor, Maurice Sterne, Boardman Robinson, George Biddle, and Reginald Marsh, grace the walls of these buildings. Two of Poor's murals created for the Justice Department Building, "Benefits of the Tennessee Valley Authority" and a triptych, "Entrance Into Prison, Vocational Training, and Release From Prison," are typical in showing the accomplishments of the New Deal or conveying a social message. As a photographer in his early twenties, Volkmar Wentzel came to know Henry Varnum Poor through his friendship with Wall Street broker and artist Edward Bruce and his wife, Peggy. It was Bruce who convinced Roosevelt to devote one percent of the construction costs of the New Deal buildings to public art works. Bruce, who became the head of the New Deal art projects, directed the planning for the murals in the Federal Triangle buildings.[25]

To display the original Declaration of Independence and the Constitution, architect John Russell Pope designed a massive semicircular rotunda as a part of the National Archives Building. Those documents were moved here for permanent exhibition from the Library of Congress in 1948. In the mid-1930s, artist Harry Faulkner painted two large murals for the rotunda portraying the historical figures present at the signing of these two historic documents.[26] Fortunately, the massive collection of paintings and sculptures remains intact today.

In addition to this unique early 20th-century American art collection, quotations which reflect the importance of the government agencies housed in each structure embellish the exterior walls of all the buildings. Workers carved the longest and perhaps the most interesting inscription around the intablature of the two curved wings of the Post Office Department Building. This inscription was written in 1851 by Joseph Holt, then Postmaster General, in true Victorian prose: "The Post Office Department, in its ceaseless labors, pervades every channel of commerce and every theatre of human enterprise, and while visiting, as it does kindly, every fireside, mingles with the throbbings of almost every heart in the land. In the multitude of its beneficence it ministers to all climes, and creeds, and pursuits, with the same fullness of fidelity. It is a delicate ear trump through which alike nations and families and isolated individuals whisper their joys and their sorrows, their convictions and their sympathies, to all who listen for their coming."[27]

## POMP AND CIRCUMSTANCE

The design of grand interiors within the Federal Triangle buildings greatly increased the pomp and circumstance of the federal government. Postal officials from across the country are sworn into office in the enormous Postmaster General's reception room, lined in mahogany paneling and lighted by crystal chandeliers. The impressive Andrew Mellon Auditorium on Constitution Avenue, with a seating capacity of 3,000, boasts gilded paneling and spectacular fifty-foot-tall fluted columns. The great reception room within the Commerce Department Building awes visitors with its coffered and gilded ceiling. Sculptors embellished the grand auditorium within the Justice Department Building with striking allegorical aluminum statues relating to the execution of justice in American courts. Businesspeople from across the country and the world who have appointments with federal officials in these edifices were and are still impressed.

The paintings, murals, and sculptures commissioned by the federal government to embellish the Federal Triangle buildings constitute the most important collection of public art ever executed for any single building complex in the country. The International Style, which was introduced for office buildings in the United States as early as the late 1930s and which came to dominate American architecture from the late-1940s until the mid-1970s, caused the developers to shun classical architecture, exemplified by the Federal Triangle, for a period of thirty-five years. The Federal Triangle remains one of the most important design and construction projects in the history of the country. The development of the complex involved several thousand people who worked on it from its inception in 1926 until the last work, the Oscar Straus Memorial Fountain, was installed on 14th Street opposite the Commerce Department Building in 1947.

Mr. Wentzel created one of the most haunting nighttime images with his Speed Graphic camera when he captured on film the statue *Guardianship* silhouetted against the floodlit Corinthian columns of the National Archives' south portico. This massive eight-foot-tall limestone male figure signifies vigilance rather than aggression. *Guardianship* holds the helmet of protection in one hand, while the other hand clasps a sheathed sword and the *fasces*, symbol of the strength and authority of government. Sculptor James Earl Fraser decorated the base supporting *Guardianship* with low-relief carvings of weapons and other martial emblems. The inscription on the front of the base, shown in the lower left corner of the photograph and attributed to Thomas Jefferson, reads: "Eternal Vigilance is the Price of Liberty."[28]

In addition to the Guardianship statue, Mr. Wentzel captured many other Washington sculptures on film after dark, including three at Scott Circle—the equestrian statue of General Winfield Scott, Daniel Webster, and the Dr. Samuel Hahnemann Memorial; the elegant Dupont Memorial Fountain by Daniel Chester French at Dupont Circle; the equestrian statue of General James McPherson in McPherson Square; the seated Lincoln in the Lincoln Memorial; the Supreme Court pediments; and the Joseph Darlington Fountain at Judiciary Square.

## NEW CONSTRUCTION ON CAPITOL HILL

The Supreme Court Building, which opened in 1935, represents the preeminent monumental government building built on Capitol Hill during the decade. Cass Gilbert's design, selected by Chief Justice William Howard Taft, included a temple with two massive side wings, each with its own large interior open-air courtyard. Its design was based directly on Leo von Klenze's early 19th-century Glyptothek in Munich—a museum of Greek sculpture.[29] Two rows of eight Corinthian fluted columns support the great portico at the front, or western, end of the temple. Volkmar Wentzel captured the monumental character of this portico, with its sculptured pediment "Equal Justice Under Law." Both the sculptured pediment and the great bronze doors on the east portray the evolution of justice and law.

Other nearby Capitol Hill construction projects completed by the government during the decade include the Adams Building of the Library of Congress, the last wing of the Russell Senate Office Building, the Longworth House Office Building, the plaza between the Capitol and Union Station, and the Botanic Garden at the west foot of the Capitol. During this construction mania Congress even voted itself $2.5 million to centrally air condition the Capitol, the Senate Office Building, and the two House Office Buildings.

The government continued to build in the nearby Southwest section of the city several colossal new projects: the Bureau of Engraving and Printing Annex, the South Building of the Agriculture Department (with 4,292 rooms it was considered the largest office building in the nation until the construction of the Pentagon five years later), the Census Building (now in use as the Ford House Office Building), the Social Security Building, the Railroad Retirement Building, and the Central Heating Plant.[30] Many other federal construction projects in the 1930s were scattered across the city.[31] New Deal agencies even built a number of public housing projects.[32]

## CLASSICAL VERSUS INTERNATIONAL STYLE

By the end of the 1930s a battle royal ensued between the traditionalists who favored the continuation of the classical mode for Washington's government buildings versus the progressive modernists, such as Frank Lloyd Wright. The last two classical buildings built on the Mall, the elegant marble National Gallery of Art and the Jefferson Memorial, created a national controversy. Both were designed by John Russell Pope and built in 1937–1941. Many architects roundly attacked both of these designs as archaic and called for the use of the International Style instead. The modernist design proposed by the Smithsonian Institution for its art gallery in 1939 at Independence Avenue and 7th Street, S.W., created an even greater uproar. This new design, won by Eliel Saarinen in a competition with eight other architects, so shocked traditionalists at the time that the Smithsonian put it on hold. It was never built because of the United States' entry into World War II. The original model and drawings, now in the possession of the Smithsonian, testify to its elegance and advanced design. Today the National Air and Space Museum, opened in 1976, occupies the site.

Franklin D. Roosevelt, more than any president except Thomas Jefferson, took a deep personal interest in the architecture of Washington and represented a driving force behind the building program of the 1930s. He consistently favored modern or simplified classical designs over the more "radical" and daring International Style. During the decade he conferred with many architects on the design of new federal buildings and monuments designed for the Washington area.[33] Roosevelt dictated the tower design for the Bethesda Naval Hospital and the simplified classical design of the new Interior Department Building. He changed Bennett's ornately detailed Apex Building at the eastern end of the Federal Triangle to a much simpler and more streamlined design. The president rejected the all-glass International Style National Airport terminal by architect Charles Goodman and directed the redesign to incorporate eight square piers based on the portico of Mount Vernon—his favorite building in the Washington area. Roosevelt often relied on advice from his friend Waddy Wood, a prominent Washington architect, whom he selected to design the Interior Department Building.[34]

## TRAFFIC

The renaming of B Street, N.W. and B Street, S.W. by Congress to the more dignified Constitution Avenue and Independence Avenue in 1931 contributed to the dignity of the Mall.[35] The widening of both of these major arteries shortly after their renaming added to their prestige. This development was an early indication that the 1930s would soon become the first decade in which automobile traffic became a serious problem. By 1939 one out of four Washington-area residents owned a car. Only Los Angeles had a higher ratio.[36] Local newspapers by mid-decade began reporting on the city's frequent massive rush-hour traffic jams. This problem resulted in major changes by city planners who attempted to improve traffic flow.

Unfortunately, the city government by the late 1930s began to widen many downtown commercial arteries, including K Street, resulting in the loss of hundreds of trees as well as the parkways between sidewalks and streets.[37] One of the tragic losses in mid-decade was the handsome flight of stone steps on the south portico of the Greek Revival Patent Office Building, demolished to widen F Street. Tunnels were built under Scott Circle, Thomas Circle, and Dupont Circle between 1937 and 1941.[38] Again, more trees came down, but the city did not replant them. Furthermore many of the residents of these historic downtown neighborhoods abandoned their houses amid the greatly increased traffic congestion and noise. Many of these historic houses were subsequently razed for commercial development, hotels, or modern apartment houses.

In addition to widening streets the city government received considerable federal funds for its own construction projects. A dozen new handsome bridges improved the appearance of the city's leading streets, including Massachusetts Avenue, Connecticut Avenue, 16th Street, P Street, and Calvert Street. Plans also got underway in 1939 to build the Baltimore-Washington Parkway but the interruption of World War II delayed its completion until 1954. Using $6 million of Works Progress Administration funds, the District commissioners in 1939 began constructing the Municipal Building on John Marshall Place just north of Pennsylvania Avenue. Nathan C. Wyeth, the municipal architect, designed it in a stripped classical mode similar to the two municipal court buildings erected at the same time on the east and west sides of Judiciary Square.

## PRIVATE CLASSICS

A number of monumental private buildings contributed to the classical appearance of Washington that emerged in the 1930s. Architect Paul Cret's Folger Shakespeare Library, built with white marble, opened in 1932. A series of sculptured relief panels by John Gregory portraying scenes from Shakespeare's plays embellishes the front facade on East Capitol Street, S.E. between 2nd and 3rd Streets. Hundreds of Depression-era workmen built a noteworthy mixture of private and government classical buildings along the west end of Constitution Avenue. These included the 1932 Public Health Service Building (now the Bureau of Indian Affairs) by J. H. deSibour at 19th Street; the 1937 Federal Reserve Building by Paul Cret at 20th Street; and the 1933 American Pharmaceutical Association Building by John

Russell Pope at 22nd Street. In addition, Pope's impressive Constitution Hall for the Daughters of the American Revolution opened in 1930 nearby on 18th Street.[39] One of the most prominent privately-owned classical commercial buildings was the Standard Oil Building at Pennsylvania Avenue and 3rd Street. Built in 1931 from the designs of Baltimore architects Fritz & Fritz, this six-story white marble structure housed offices as well as the city's largest auto garage. This landmark was unfortunately razed in 1968 for the construction of the intercity beltway, which was never built. The Labor Department Building occupies the site today.

Three important new classically inspired private churches included the National Baptist Church by Egerton Swartwout and the Mormon Church by Young and Hansen, both built in 1933 at 16th Street and Columbia Road, and the massive National City Christian Church by John Russell Pope at Thomas Circle. The District of Columbia Red Cross Building at 18th and E Streets also opened in the 1930s.

## LASTING LEGACY

The great federal building program that transformed Washington from provincial backwater to international arena can be judged today in two lights. To some people it may seem ironic that the "federal establishment" built a fabulously costly and extravagant capital at the expense of millions of Americans with low incomes struggling to survive during the Depression. Trappings of grandeur found in the classical porticos as well as the elegant interior spaces reserved for cabinet members and ceremonial purposes fueled public criticism. Many compared the massive building program in Washington to Adolf Hitler's grand new public buildings in Berlin or Mussolini's gigantic new architectural stage settings in Rome. Some even said the design for the Federal Reserve Building on Constitution Avenue was stolen from Albert Speer's plans for the rebuilding of Nuremberg.

Historians, however, often wait a considerable length of time to evaluate important developments. To me it seems that after fifty years, we can now look back on the 1930s and judge the developments that made Washington a monumental city. The extensive construction program, initiated in the late 1920s during prosperity and accelerated under the New Deal as a means of providing jobs and improving the economy, set the stage for postwar America. That stage was first used for the state visit of King George VI and Queen Elizabeth in June 1939. They came to seek American aid as the British prepared for war with Germany. The resulting newsreels, shown in movie theaters across the country and around the world, gave the world its first glimpse of Washington's new monumentality.

Pearl Harbor triggered the changes that made Washington the center of the world stage and changed its pace decisively. With the end of World War II the city of Washington became the power center of the Free World. The city was now a fitting place to receive world leaders and for the dignified display of the artifacts of our culture in public museums. The building program of the 1930s continued the original classical designs fostered by the country's founders and successfully unified the architectural design of the nation's capital. The solid value of the dollar during the Depression enabled the government to use the finest of construction materials while giving jobs to thousands. Indeed, the General Services Administration, entrusted with most of the design and construction of federal government buildings, today could never approach the quality of materials and workmanship used in pre-World War II Washington.

We are all fortunate indeed that Volkmar Wentzel arrived in Washington in 1935, elected to stay, and learned the art of photography. He created a unique and mystical record of "Washington by Night"—here seen for the first time in over fifty years!

## NOTES

The author thanks the following for offering suggestions for improving the style and contents of the introduction: Mark Andrich, Amy Ballard, Kenneth Bowling, Robin de Silva, Judy Frank, Howard Gillette, Amy Henderson, Sue Kohler, Richard Longstreth, Virginia McPeak, William Walleck, and Myra Wilson.

1. Recent research has shown that L'Enfant Anglicized his first name to Peter shortly after he arrived in America during the Revolution. He continued to use the name Peter rather than Pierre throughout his life in the United States.
2. Marie Beale, *Decatur House and Its Inhabitants* (Washington, D.C.: National Trust for Historic Preservation, 1954), p. 134.
3. The Bonus Act of 1924 stipulated that all American military veterans of World War I would be paid a bonus in 1945 of $1 per day for duty in the United States and $1.25 per day for duty overseas. Marchall McNeil, "House Passage of Patman Bill Brought Bonus March," *Washington Daily News*, July 9, 1963.
4. John Henry Bartlett, *The Bonus March and the New Deal* (Chicago: M.A. Donohue and Co, 1937), p. 97.
5. Jerry Oppenheimer, "Government Boomtown," *Washington Daily News*, November 8, 1971.
6. "Washington is Having Best Year Since 1929," *Washington Daily News*, September 1, 1936.
7. W.M. Kiplinger, *Washington Is Like That* (New York: Harper & Bro., 1942), pp. 6–7, 97–98, 123.
8. Oliver McKee, Jr. "Washington as a Boom Town," *North American Review*, February 1935, p. 179.
9. "U.S. Capital: Cross Section of America," *Christian Science Monitor*, April 18, 1938.
10. "Washington Is Having the Best Year Since 1929," *Washington Daily News*, September 5, 1936.
11. Frederick G. Vosburgh, "Wonders of the New Washington," *National Geographic Magazine*, 1935, p. 488.
12. John Chabot Smith, "First Frost Leaves Trail of Glory," *Washington Post*, October 20, 1939.
13. It would not be until the 1950s, however, that the George Washington Parkway was extended from Arlington National Cemetery to the present site of the Beltway.
14. Frances Parkinson Keyes, "Capital Kaleidoscope," *Cosmopolitan*, July 1937, p. 49.
15. Glenn S. Orlin, "The Evolution of the American Urban Parkway," Ph.D. dissertation, American Civilization, George Washington University, 1992, pp. 225–226.
16. Christine Sadler, "Story of 1939: a Great Capital Grows Greater," *Evening Star*, December 30, 1939.
17. "Report of the Chronicler," *Records of the Columbia Historical Society* (Washington, D.C.: Columbia Historical Society, 1940), Vols.40–41, p. 259.
18. "Report of the Chronicler," *Records of the Columbia Historical Society* (Washington, D.C.: Columbia Historical Society, 1935), Vols. 35–36, p. 328.
19. Constance McLaughlin Green, *Washington, Capital City, 1879–1950* (Princeton, N.J.: Princeton University Press, 1963), Vol. II, p. 395.
20. Secretary of the Treasury Andrew Mellon directed the site planning and design of the buildings in the new complex. His careful attention to detail and insistence on high-quality construction materials influenced the monumentality of these buildings. To secure the very best designs possible, the American Institute of Architects (AIA) lobbied for the participation of private architectural firms rather than the traditional Office of the Supervising Architect of the Treasury. The AIA argued successfully that finer and more harmonious designs would result.

21. Sue A. Kohler, *The Commission of Fine Arts, a Brief History, 1910–1990*, (Washington, D.C.: Commission of Fine Arts, 1990), p. 199.
22. Building projects in both Europe and America also influenced the design and planning of Federal Triangle. Important prototypes in Europe were the planning of Regent Street and Regent's Park by John Nash in the 1820s in London, Baron Haussmann's rebuilding of Paris for Napoleon III in the 1850s, and the redesign of the core of Vienna in the 1860s. In the United States, influence came from the design of the World's Fair in Chicago in 1893 with its committee of architects who coordinated planning. Frederick Gutheim, *Worthy of the Nation, The History of Planning for the National Capitol* (Washington, D.C. : Smithsonian Institution Press, 1977), p. 175.
23. Alan Balfour, *Rockfeller Center, Architecture as Theater* (New York: McGraw-Hill, 1978), pp. vii–viii.
24. George Gurney, *Sculpture and the Federal Triangle* (Washington, D.C.: Smithsonian Institution Press, 1985), pp. 1–5
25. *Ibid*, pp. 292–293.
26. *Washington, City and Capital, Federal Writers' Project* (Washington, D.C.: Government Printing Office, 1937), p. 994.
27. James M. Goode, *The Outdoor Sculpture of Washington, D.C., a Comprehensive Historical Guide* (Washington, D.C.: Smithsonian Institution Press, 1974), p. 165.
28. *Ibid*, p. 151.
29. William A Millen, "City Leading Government Center of World," *Evening Star*, October 11, 1936.
30. "Actual Work Near on 3 Projects in Southwest Area," *Evening Star*, September 17, 1939.
31. Daniel L. Cohn, "Washington the Blest," *Atlantic Monthly*, May 1939, p. 611.
32. James M. Goode, *Best Addresses, a Century of Washington's Distinguished Apartment Houses* (Washington, D.C.: Smithsonian Institution Press, 1988) pp. 337–338.
33. Benjamin Forgey, "FDR's Grand Designs," *Washington Post*, October 11, 1982.
34. The president had Wood draw up plans to remodel the massive, Second Empire-style State, War, and Navy Building (now the Old Executive Office Building), in the classical mode to match the Treasury Department Building but never carried out the plans because of the interruption of World War II. Inspired by Andrew Jackson as the founder of the Democratic party, Roosevelt further commissioned Wood to design the 1937 inaugural reviewing stand in front of the White House as a replica of the Hermitage, Jackson's Greek Revival Tennessee plantation house. William B. Rhoads, "Franklin D. Roosevelt and Washington Architecture," *Records of the Columbia Historical Society* (Washington, D.C.: Columbia Historical Society, 1989), Vol. 52, p. 106.
35. "Report of the Chronicler," *Records of the Columbia Historical Society* (Washington, D.C.: Columbia Historical Society, 1934), Vols. 37–38, p. 227.
36. Leo A. Borah, "Washington, Home City and Show Place," *National Geographic Society*, June 1937, p. 668.
37. "Washington—Our City Beautiful," *American Motorist*, November 1939, p. 17.
38. "Report of the Chronicler," *Records of the Columbia Historical Society* (Washington, D.C.: Columbia Historical Society, 1944), Vol. 44–45, p. 341.
39. Constitution Hall made national headlines in 1939 when the Daughters of the American Revolution refused to allow the famous black contralto Marian Anderson to sing in the auditorium. Consequently Secretary of the Interior Harold Ickes authorized her to use the Lincoln Memorial on the Mall, and an audience of more than 75,000 people listened to her sing there on Easter Sunday, 1939.

# LAFAYETTE SQUARE

ANDREW Jackson's silhouette is unmistakably 19th-century American: the tip of the hat, the ramrod posture. The cockade of hair above the brow is recognizably Jacksonian. (Compare his forelock in the Sully portrait on a $20 bill.) Jackson's horse rears up from a plain granite oval, inscribed "Jackson" and "The Federal Union, It Must Be Preserved." The quote was from Jackson's toast at the 1830 Jefferson Day Dinner; Jackson was warning others to check threats of Southern secession over a tariff that favored New England mercantile enterprise over Southern agriculture.

The cannons on either side of the statue, cast in the Spanish royal foundry at Barcelona between 1743 and 1776, were seized by Jackson at Pensacola during the Indian Wars. This was the first equestrian statue cast in the United States. Sculptor Clark Mills's 1850 work shows Jackson reviewing his troops after his triumph at the Battle of New Orleans.

Equestrian statues of military leaders are a tradition as old as time, but this portrayal of horse and rider is singularly apt, for Jackson raised horses in Tennessee and raced them in Washington, sometimes under the name of Rachel Jackson's nephew, A. J. Donelson. Congress adjourned for races at the track east of Washington Circle.

As Jackson's raised hat acknowledges his troops, so the North Portico of the White House, which frames the statue in this photograph is an architectural salute to Old Hickory himself. The pediment supported by eight Doric columns was rushed to completion in 1829 to ornament the presidential mansion's previously flat front facade, just in time for the famously rowdy inauguration of America's first frontier president.

Elected as a man of the people, Jackson was nevertheless accorded a royal, if roistering, reception. Upstate New York farmers marked the great occasion by sending a wagon weighted down with several tons of cheddar. The Great Cheese lingered as an enormous presence just inside the front door of the White House foyer. After many months the general public was allowed to step inside the North Portico to carve off snacks. It vanished in a morning, but the grease spot lingered on.

# ST. JOHN'S CHURCH

ARTIFICIAL illumination exaggerates the simple but compelling decorations on the exterior of St. John's Church on Lafayette Square at 16th and H Streets. The plain demeanor of this structure expressed the religious beliefs of the architect, Benjamin Henry Latrobe. He perceived the church as a place for preaching, and believed it should be unencumbered by decoration. Members of Latrobe's family were leaders in the Moravian church in England (although his mother was born in Montgomery County, Pennsylvania). Latrobe studied engineering in Germany and architecture in London.

This church was the second important structure to go up around the president's park, the White House having been started in 1792. Earlier, a family graveyard of the Pearces (early proprietors) and an apple orchard had covered the spot. "I have just completed a church that made many Washingtonians religious who had not been religious before," noted the architect in 1816. Latrobe made a gift of his work, which included writing a hymn for the church dedication. He refused the vestry's offer of a free pew, accepting only a suitably inscribed silver goblet. The multi-talented man also served as the Church's first organist.

A pew at St. John's was also offered to the president; James Madison suggested the church committee pick it for him and, as a result, pew twenty-eight has since been known as (and very frequently used as) the President's Pew.

These excerpts from Benjamin Ogle Tayloe link the church to the house Latrobe designed for Stephen Decatur: "On the conclusion of the war of 1812, St. John's Church was the first building erected on the Square, to which my father was by far the largest contributor, and to which he presented the massive church service of silver which formerly belonged to the old church of Lunenburg in Richmond County, Virginia."

Rev. Dr. Hawley, rector for twenty-five years, was an original. In the war of 1812, he was captain of a company of volunteers, raised for the defense of the city of New York. On being ordered to the Niagara frontier with his company, composed chiefly of theological students, the captain refused to go. To avoid a court-martial, he was permitted to resign. In derision, when he became a rector, some called him "Captain Hawley." Commodore Decatur would not attend his church "because he refused to obey orders."

# DECATUR HOUSE ENTRANCE

IN THE MID-1930s, Mr. Wentzel photographed 748 Jackson Place, then-Ambassador and Mrs. Truxtun Beale's home on Lafayette Square. The ambassador died in the summer of 1936. Surviving him by nearly two decades, Mrs. Beale left the square's last private house to the National Trust for Historic Preservation. It was thenceforth called "Decatur House."

If you had said "Decatur House" to a cabby the year Mr. Wentzel shot this photograph, you would have arrived at 2812 N Street, where Stephen Decatur's widow had moved long ago, after financial embarrassment drove her from the Square's prestigious precincts to the shabby confines of Georgetown. The particulars of her removal tell a bittersweet Washington tale of fame and obscurity.

Stephen Decatur, born in Philadelphia in 1779 into a distinguished naval family, came to fame fighting the Barbary pirates. In his most celebrated adventure, he rowed stealthily by night into the harbor "on the shores of Tripoli" to burn the captured frigate *Philadelphia* to the waterline, rendering it useless to the "Barbarians." He was also a hero in the War of 1812. Decatur carried "Letters of Reprisal and Marque," which authorized private ships to pursue the enemy in the government's name and capture them for profit. Decatur spent his prize money on the first private house on Lafayette Square in 1818. Benjamin Latrobe was his architect.

Two years later Decatur died by the hand of Naval officer James Barron. During the so-called impressment outrages of 1807, (which led to the War of 1812), Barron had surrendered the *Chesapeake* to the British ship *Leopard* without resistance.

Sitting on the court martial that suspended Barron, Decatur had steadfastly resisted Barron's pleas for reinstatement. A challenge was issued and duly answered at the Bladensburg dueling ground.

To avoid encountering either the survivor or the seconder in the fatal duel, Susan Wheeler Decatur withdrew from society, pinched by means too slender to support her earlier style. She rented her house to the French minister and his wife, the Baroness Hyde de Neuville. Raising cash by selling off family treasures, she wrote President Jackson, "I am literally without a dollar to send to market, and am living upon the patience and kindness of my Butcher and Baker."

The widow converted to Roman Catholicism; gossips claimed she hoped to marry the rich Charles Carroll, last surviving signer of the Declaration of Independence. There was no marriage; he died in 1832. Whatever its spiritual dimension, her conversion was the key to her annuity from Georgetown University. The Jesuits, needing cash for the school, eagerly accepted from the frail widow in her fifties what was left of the Decatur fortune. Surviving into her nineties, she died in 1860; her initial capital had by then been recouped several times over.

# DECATUR HOUSE

IN 1872, a Washington widow privately printed a memorial volume, *Our Neighbors on La Fayette Square, Anecdotes and Reminiscences* that included some of a memoir by Benjamin Ogle Tayloe and a diagram of Lafayette Park. A key lists the houses on the square and their occupants, past and (then) present. The list is not complete, but is useful all the same. For the house facing the park's northwest corner, at the corner of Jackson Place and H Street, the key lists these occupants: "Commodore Stephen Decatur; Henry Clay; Martin Van Buren, Vice-president; John Gadsby; Edward Livingston, Secretary of State; George M. Dallas, Vice-president; General Beale (present occupant)." This last named man was the rich San Franciscan, General Edward Fitzgerald Beale. More than fifty years later, when Mr. Wentzel took this photograph through the door of what is now called Decatur House, the son of "General Beale (present occupant)" was still in residence.

Truxtun Beale, son of the general, was born in San Francisco in 1866. His sister married John R. McLean of the Cincinnati steamship and publishing fortune and longtime owner of the *Washington Post*. In 1891, Beale went to Persia as U.S. Minister, serving afterwards in Greece, Romania, and Serbia. He first married Harriet Blaine, daughter of "the plumed knight of American politics," James G. Blaine, who built the red brick house still standing just off Dupont Circle. After a divorce, he married a grandniece of Salmon P. Chase, Marie Oge of San Rafael, California.

He was in New York in 1906, on the roof of Madison Square Garden with Pittsburgh playboy Harry Thaw and his showgirl wife, Evelyn Nesbit. Evelyn Walsh McLean (the wife of Beale's nephew) wrote in *Father Struck it Rich*: "Suddenly Uncle Trux heard something pop; people jumped to their feet, women screamed. Just then the young husband came back and said, 'Here, Truxtun, you take Evelyn home. I've just shot Stanford White.' In his hand was a pistol that still exhaled a burned-powder odor.

"Uncle Trux was petrified. He was still, he hoped, a person eligible for diplomatic honors, and there he found himself smack in the middle of a page-one scandal. "Uncle Trux was not feeling gallant then; he hustled Evelyn Nesbit down to the street, boosted her into a taxi cab, and himself raced off to catch a train for California . . . Uncle Trux never came back across the Rockies until the trial was over, and Harry Thaw was safe in an asylum." Mrs. McLean loved to twit her in-laws. She noted that Uncle Trux had a short fuse: "Once, on Marie's behalf, he shot a California editor." "Marie Oge Beale is very handsome, as vivid as a poppy," observed Mrs. McLean. She recounted her husband's tale of being summoned to H Street and 17th, where George von Lengerke Meyer, Taft's Secretary of the Navy, and Truxtun Beale were "fighting in front of the Metropolitan Club. They began by pulling each other's noses on the club steps, and now they are locked together rolling in the gutter. The House Committee thinks I ought to come and separate 'em."

# DECATUR HOUSE H STREET

WHEN Volkmar Kurt Wentzel found lodgings on Jackson Place in the 30s, Lafayette Square still bore traces of having once been the city's premier stylish residential neighborhood, though by then its "institutional" character was dominant. He remembers well an afternoon visit to his garret by the distinguished founding fathers of the National Gallery of Art. "One by one, huffing and puffing," he relates, "Andrew Mellon, Nicolas Brown (father of J. Carter Brown), David Finley, John Walker, and John Russell Pope, I think, appeared at the balustrade of my top floor landing. Pointing with his cane, Mr. Mellon asked me if they could have a look out of my dormer window, which indeed they did. Next to my spartan cot, they took turns peering out and commenting about the beauty of the view. One month later, all the occupants of 716 received notices to move. The property had been bought by Andrew Mellon, and shortly afterward became the headquarters for the building of the National Gallery of Art."

In 1906, Henry Adams had proclaimed "La Fayette Square was society." In the 1930s any casual observer could still see what he meant. It never meant isolation. While there was strict segregation and social stratification, living in "society" here never meant living apart. It was rich and poor, black and white, jumbled close together from the start. Today's Washington is far less residentially integrated, either by race or by income.

While Lafayette Square was lined with fine houses, there were also such modest structures as the one Mr. Wentzel photographed, a long two-story servants' wing stretching west along H Street behind Decatur House. Though humble, it has a magical gleam, mysteriously pulling in light from the darkness. Who sits in the doorway? Whose lights are in the windows? What is the source of illumination of leaves at the top of the photograph?

This structure is noted in the 1937 city guide compiled by the Federal Writers' Project of the Works Progress Administration, calling "the Decatur house which still stands at 748 Jackson Place one of the few original houses to survive and probably the least changed." The book gives a brief account of Decatur and finds his house "singularly like him in character."

It continues, "For a brief but regrettable period, about 1844, John Gadsby leased the property and made the garden at the rear of the house into a slave market, protected from sight by an 8-foot brick wall on the south and an ell adjoining the house on the H Street side. The ell, a long one-story brick building, its windows barred with iron, was used as a corral for Negro slaves. That and the original garden wall still stand."

You can see that the ell was two storys, not one. And the "slave pen" legend seems to be hearsay. But surely the humble ell stands as a poignant contrast to Latrobe's corner structure.

# BELASCO THEATER

**A**T THIS HOUR of the night, Lafayette Square appears deserted except for one stylish couple seated on a bench. The park seems, however, to have been planned to accommodate substantial crowds, if we can judge by the width of the walk that directs our eyes toward the ghostly neon glimmering at the Belasco Theater. Looming to the right of the theater, across an unseen Pennsylvania Avenue, is the U.S. Treasury.

The Belasco is long gone but fondly remembered by many who knew Washington during the bustling days of World War II, when it housed the Stagedoor Canteen. This U.S.O. facility opened in the fall of 1942 as the official morale builder for servicemen with time on their hands. Volunteering to jolly up our boys in the military was *the* thing for civic-minded Washingtonians to do. Men dished out the java and slung hash, washing up afterwards; the women cut a friendly rug on the dance floor or helped a bashful farm boy find a stamp to write a letter home to Mom.

Local people who gave their time to the U.S.O. at the Belasco rewarded themselves with an inner smile of recognition whenever they heard the sentimental Tin Pan Alley favorite that began "I left my heart at the Stagedoor Canteen."

Not surprisingly, Hollywood cranked out scores of movies about "the war effort." *Stagedoor Canteen* was a big hit, with a string of celebrities making cameo appearances in this story of chance meetings and farewells; it was not a movie about the wartime festivities at the Belasco but about such facilities in general. Still, it had a special meaning to the many Washingtonians who took pride in their morale-building hours at the Belasco.

The theater was built in 1895 as the Lafayette Square Opera House. A decade later, David Belasco and the Shubert brothers took over the operation and changed the name. For many years it ranked just behind the National Theater on any list of the city's most prestigious stages; its playbills boasted the greatest names in American theater. Helen Hayes was a child of five from Mount Pleasant when she first sang before its footlights.

The diminished audiences of the mid-30s prompted the Shuberts to sell the place. Movies were shown for a while; then stage plays again. In 1940, the federal government bought the entire row of buildings along Madison Place facing the park, using the Belasco as extra space for the Treasury.

The Belasco was razed in 1964. Today, the United States Court of Claims stands on the site.

# OLD COSMOS CLUB

MR. WENTZEL must have crossed Lafayette Square from his Jackson Place garret one evening and used his camera to peek into the window of the Cosmos Club, capturing in silhouette this small statue of Lafayette by Paul Bartlett. This window was in the part of the club lodged in a building at that time second in from the intersection of H Street and Madison Place. Over the years, the club occupied several houses in a line from that corner.

The Cosmos Club's organizational meeting was held in November 1878, at the home of its prime mover, Major John Wesley Powell, second director of the U.S. Geological Survey (and probably best known for his explorations of the Grand Canyon). The club moved to No. 23 Lafayette Square (or Madison Place) in 1882; four years later it acquired the house on the corner, built in 1818 by Congressman Richard Cutts, whose wife was Dolley Madison's sister. James Madison bought this house in 1828. After he died in 1836, his widow lived there until she died in 1849. In 1851 it was purchased by Admiral Charles Wilkes, controversial leader of the 1838–1842 "Exploratory Expedition." It was from his widow, Mary, that the Cosmos Club bought it in 1886. In 1890, a side entrance was created so that such groups as the National Geographic Society could enter the building without disturbing club members; this task was spearheaded by G. Brown Goode, cousin of James Goode.

The club's success led to further real estate acquisitions and upgrades, going down the block toward the Treasury. In 1909, the structures at No. 23 and No. 25 were demolished and a five-story building erected: this is the one Mr. Wentzel photographed here.

In 1917, the Cosmos Club acquired the residence of Benjamin Ogle Tayloe, whose memoir is quoted in the caption on page twenty-four. In its post-Tayloe years, the house known as No. 21 belonged to Senator Don Cameron of Pennsylvania, Vice President Garret Hobart, and Senator Mark Hanna of Ohio. Tayloe was famous for his hospitable ways, and it seems fitting that the Tayloe stretch of this block is accessible to the public as a cafeteria serving the U.S. Court of Claims, which now sprawls down Madison Place, looming behind the small-scale structures of past decades.

The Cosmos Club left Madison Place in the 1950s and moved to its present site on Massachusetts Avenue between R and Florida. Improbably, it has maintained its scholarly aura even there. The Cosmos Club's seriousness of purpose was diminished not one whit in the outrageously rich surroundings of the Townsend house. There the dashing Mathilde Townsend Gerry Welles who once caused scandal by smoking cigarettes and divorcing, had in earlier decades dazzled *tout Washington* with the Youssoupouf black pearls around her neck. The Cosmos Club's walls have always been hung thick with prize-winning scientists and writers, but since it departed Lafayette Square for Massachusetts Avenue, the ceilings of its grand headquarters can only be characterized as "off-the-wall" opulent.

# ALEXANDER HAMILTON

H IS BACK to the Treasury's south entrance, Alexander Hamilton cuts a dashing figure, for sculptor James Earle Fraser modelled him as notably manly and vigorous. Legend claims that Charles Atlas posed for it. The full-muscled calf beneath the hose reminds us that "Spindleshanks" was an 18th-century insult.

The ten-foot bronze Hamilton stands on marble cornered with *fasces*, most appropriate for a first secretary of the treasury committed to a powerful central government. From the word *fasces* comes "fascism." This bundle of sticks, signifying authority since Roman times, is best known to us as the emblem on the "mercury dime." We've used the *fasces* symbol since "dime" was spelled "disme."

Chiseled below is Daniel Webster's ringing 1831 tribute to Hamilton: "He smote the rock of the national resources and abundant streams of revenue gushed forth. He touched the dead corpse of the public credit and it sprang upon its feet."

This must have seemed miraculous to Webster, who had lifelong money troubles and never got the hang of the mercantile system.

Although Hamilton was not a local resident, Washington needs him in bronze; without him, none of us might be here. The compromise whereby the nation's capital was situated here was a byproduct of Hamilton's fiscal policies. The thirteen colonies had incurred varying degrees of debt in the break from Britain. If the newly united states assumed these debts *en masse*, the most populous state (Virginia, which owed but little) must shoulder the greatest burden. In the heaviest debtor state, New York, money men had gambled on an "aye" outcome, buying up state notes speculating they would be fully redeemed by the federal government. In short, the North had more to gain from assumption; the South would be the loser.

Equally thorny was the issue of where to put the seat of the federal government. While every jurisdiction wanted this political plum for its own enrichment, each felt that unless it could be tucked in his *own* back pocket, it was an error to put it where an existing political establishment could bully the fledgling Republic's legislators. The solution was a new city. But where? George Washington's prestige backed a new capital on the Potomac, a site far south of the demographic center of the nation.

Thomas Jefferson had just returned from Paris when Hamilton buttonholed him: the new union was in danger of foundering on the rock of assumption. Writing of this crisis two years later, Jefferson observed that "as the pill would be a bitter one to Southern States, something should be done to soothe them, that the removal of the seat of Government to the Patowmac [sic] was a just measure, & would probably be a popular one with them and would be a proper one to follow assumption."

Thus occurred Washington, D.C. The debts had only begun.

# PENNSYLVANIA AVENUE

THROUGH metal gates (now gone) at the Treasury Building, we're looking straight down Pennsylvania Avenue to the Capitol dome on a winter night in 1937 with just enough snow to look pretty but not enough to cover the street car tracks. This same vista in springtime appears in the 1991 District of Columbia Bicentennial stamp, not nearly so well composed as Mr. Wentzel's work. His slow exposure turns homeward-bound automobiles into rivulets of light. Note the line of cars at right: no snow emergency regulations in 1937.

At right looms the Old Post Office's tower, at 315 feet of gray granite the city's third most visible landmark. Designed by Willoughby J. Edbrooke in the Romanesque style of H. H. Richardson, it was begun in 1892 and finished in 1899, just in time for pained looks from enthusiasts of the neoclassical "City Beautiful" movement. If Treasury coffers had been more full, the post office would surely have been replaced. The Old Post Office was the first federal building constructed between the Treasury and the Capitol; it was not until the 20th century that Pennsylvania Avenue became the main stem of our monumental core. Since World War I, and particularly in the 1930s, the government has raised enormous structures, which have replaced small shops and businesses that once lined the avenue.

The connection between the Capitol and the White House is Washington's ceremonial route. Here at war's conclusion the armies pass in review; here the inaugural parades mark the change of command. Aesthetes have worried endlessly about the dogleg in Pennsylvania Avenue that marches to the Treasury, wheels to the right up 15th Street for a couple of blocks, then reappears after a left turn toward Lafayette Square and the White House.

The Champs Elysee doesn't hop about like that.

People like to blame the roundabout route on the decisive and hot-tempered Andrew Jackson. Said to have grown impatient with the wrangle over just where the new Treasury should go (the old one was uphill and much smaller), he banged his stick along 15th Street and said, "Put it here."

True or not, some apologists say it was a good thing. L'Enfant originally planned a much larger, more imperial presidential palace; when political wisdom decreed a smaller one, the axes were skewed anyway. So Pennsylvania Avenue has to jig around.

# U.S. CAPITOL

SQUARES of rain on the plaza at the base of the Library of Congress's ceremonial stair form a murky mirror to reflect street lights and the Capitol dome. Particularly striking is the dome's double image, crystal clear with every column distinct as it soars into the night sky above, while the reflected dome below is blurred but still recognizable in a netherworld of paving squares and rain water.

This dark and light version is a nice metaphor for the way government works. What's the lesson here? That all soaring precision is undergirded with ephemeral murk? Which dome is real, which is the illusion?

Look at the upper image to consider, as a case in point, the finial called *Freedom* that tops the U.S. Capitol dome. This statue depicts the classically-draped figure of a woman, almost twenty feet high, sculpted by Thomas Crawford (1814–1857), an American who, like many 19th-century sculptors, worked in Rome. From Italy, he shipped back the plaster model; the statue itself was cast in bronze by slave labor at Clark Mills's Bladensburg foundry.

Crawford was well known because, in 1840, he won the prestigious commission to sculpt the equestrian statue of George Washington that is in Richmond; a statue of Crawford himself is there at the Virginia Museum of Fine Arts. Though he lived out his life far from his native New York, Crawford's career was, nevertheless, touched by America's mid-century turmoils.

For one thing, his wife's sister was Julia Ward Howe, who wrote that most stirring of Civil War anthems, "The Battle Hymn of the Republic," while in a hotel room at the Willard.

For another, his first version of *Freedom* showed the woman wearing the Phrygian Cap (also called the Liberty Cap) which in ancient Roman times signified a freed slave. It was famed as an emblem during the French Revolution.

When the design of *Freedom* with her highly-charged headgear became known, it caused a great brouhaha. Since in those days all federal buildings were the provenance of the Army Engineering Corps, this statue's hat went right up to the Secretary of War, Jefferson Davis, who took umbrage at the lady's millinery as a gratuitous slap at the South's "peculiar institution."

It was Davis himself who suggested the change to a less charged (if more baffling) headdress: a helmet with a circle of stars "expressive of endless existence and heavenly birth," on top of which is an eagle's head and a burst of feathers suggestive of the ceremonial headgear of a Plains Indian.

# TRAMWAY STATION

IN 1936, Mr. Wentzel photographed two soldiers seated on a bench and identified the photograph as the "Old Tramway Station at the U.S. Capitol." He must have had the east front at his back when he took this picture, for this is a shot looking across First Street toward the Jefferson Building of the Library of Congress, where the distinctive and elaborate street lights bring to mind candelabra in full blaze.

The little structure where the soldiers sit is part of what was Frederick Law Olmsted's plan for the Capitol grounds. His designs bring down to human scale the building's dimensions. The small red brick grotto on the south side is a case in point. Olmsted planned a pair of tramway stations at which riders could wait under shelter for the arrival of the public conveyances. Horses pulled vehicles along tracks that came right up on the Capitol grounds, where the turnarounds were also located. The tramway that turned around on the Senate side took a Pennsylvania Avenue route downtown. The tramway on the House side went east toward the Anacostia River.

When streetcars became motorized the track systems changed and those around the Capitol were removed. The soldiers in Mr. Wentzel's photograph were probably not waiting for transportation but just resting up a bit, perhaps looking around at the handsome lights making pinpoints of glare in the night.

The lighting of the nation's capital was an important matter. There was an act of the corporation of the city of Washington "providing for lighting the avenues and streets" in 1803, at which time some lampposts went up along Pennsylvania Avenue. Gas was used to light local streets in 1842, two decades after Baltimore installed it. In 1842, Congress ordered lights for the city's only lighted street, Pennsylvania Avenue from the White House to the Capitol, then called "The Great National Broadway of the Metropolis." After two years they cut back to save money; the lights only burned when Congress was in session. At mid-century, more lighting was installed, but the lamps were not lit on nights when moonlight was anticipated. After the Civil War, technology improved.

In private life, Alexander Robey Shepherd was a purveyor of street lights. When, in the early 1870s, he took over the reins as governor of the District of Columbia, gas lamps were an important part of his vision of the city's transformation from war-ravaged camp to municipal showplace. His controversial administration also saw the installation of miles of underground sewers, roads regraded and paved, and the planting of trees. These were calculated both by miles of shade and numbers of trees.

# ULYSSES S. GRANT MEMORIAL

THE CAPITOL dome has drawn all the light in this photograph. Eerily, the figure of Ulysses S. Grant seems to vanish into blackness. We can barely discern the tired, calm military leader in his soft battered hat, swordless as was his habit, riding his Kentucky thoroughbred. Night's blackness swallows him before our eyes. If we look away, he might be gone from the photograph entirely. But where would he go? What happens to our statues when we don't keep an eye on them? Does Grant ride off with fellow officers among the city's other equestrian effigies?

Would his horse, Cincinnatus, respond to the whinnying of Rienzi, echoing from Phil Sheridan's Circle on 23rd and R at Massachusetts? Would they recognize the hoofbeat tattoo of John Logan's spirited horse? Would they rendezvous with William Tecumseh Sherman and his mount on Pennsylvania Avenue at Treasury Place? And would the ghostly bronze quartet return to old haunts at the White House? Grant spent eight years there, the first full two-term president since Andrew Jackson.

The Red Room turned blue with cigar smoke as Grant and his Army comrades relived the war years, reenacting its battles on the floor littered with household items. Cups were cannon emplacements, candlesticks were pushed along as troop movements, piles of books were hills. The men used neither first names nor titles, just Grant, Logan, Sherman, Sheridan. Rooms away, the women talked, calling each other Miss Julia, Miss Mary, Miss Ellen. Sheridan, much the youngest, was a bachelor until 1875; his bride was Miss Irene Rucker.

Sheridan's daughters lived on until after World War II. From their apartment window, they waved goodnight to Papa as sculpted by Gutzon Borglum. Or so the neighbors liked to say.

If the Union Army leaders should sally forth down the avenues, they would find many comrades at arms in the nation's capital where Civil War heroes are featured in circles and squares. Except for Albert Pike (briefly a Confederate general), all are Union leaders: Generals George McClellan, James McPherson, George Thomas, Winfield Scott, W.S. Hancock, John A. Rawlins, Admirals Samuel Francis Dupont and David Farragut.

Major L'Enfant himself summoned these brazen shades. Our city's first plan called for memorials: "The center of each Square will admit of Statues, Columns, Obelisks, or any other ornament such as the different States may choose to erect: to perpetuate not only the memory of such individuals whose counsels or Military achievements were conspicuous in giving liberty and independence to this Country; but also those whose usefulness hath rendered them worthy of general imitation, to invite the youth of succeeding generations to tread in the paths of those sages; or heroes whom their country has thought proper to celebrate."

# GRANT MEMORIAL ARTILLERY

TALL TREES vanish high in the black night above the Artillery Group, silhouetted against a city sky brightened by foggy overcast. It is the southern part of the Grant Memorial west of the U.S. Capitol. This is the east end of the Mall, and the Lincoln Memorial anchors the Mall's west end; planners intended to suggest the historical bond between the Civil War president and his towering military leader.

In 1895, the idea of a Grant memorial was first proposed by the Society of the Army of the Tennessee, the Union force that Grant had commanded. The Tennessee is a river. (Northerners named their forces and their battles after natural phenomena like rivers. Thus, Bull Run, a creek, is the Yankee name for the battle Southerners call Manassas, which is the name of the nearest town. Antietam (a creek) is the same battle site as Sharpsburg (a town).

Shortly after the turn of the century, Congress voted to honor Grant with one of the largest sums ever devoted to a memorial. Sculptors were invited to compete. Among the judges were McMillan Park Commission member Augustus Saint-Gaudens and Daniel Chester French (who would in time sculpt the Lincoln seated in the Memorial down the Mall). The prize went to Henry Merwin Schrady (1871–1922), outraging older and better known artists, who felt that Schrady would never have won if he had been a nobody. He was a somebody; his family was well-connected in New York and his father, Dr. George Schrady, had been the physician attending Grant as he died from cancer of the jaw.

Socialite or not, young Schrady gave it his all. He studied Grant's life mask at the Smithsonian. He posed real West Point cadets from the class of 1908, using them as models for the three men seated on the limber box. He dissected horses to master their anatomy. He wet down his equestrian model to see how muscles rippled under wet hide.

Schrady's opus, the city's largest work of statuary, was cast in Brooklyn at the Roman Bronze Foundry, owned by Ricardo Bertelli. Enormous logistical difficulties were overcome before it was dedicated on the centennial of Grant's birth, April 27, 1922. There was a grand military parade, with Grant descendants present, and speeches by General of the Armies John Pershing and Vice President Calvin Coolidge. President Harding was away dedicating Grant's birthplace near Cincinnati.

Henry Merwin Schrady was not present, either. He was dead from overwork on this astonishing technical feat, having made a life's work of creating a bronze simulacrum of war's horrors, every twig underfoot, every uniform button, moustache hair, boot strap, and bridle.

# DARLINGTON FOUNTAIN

LOST to us today is this vista Mr. Wentzel captured in the mid-1930s. Whatever structure was going up when the photograph was taken was subsequently replaced by something even larger; now between the Capitol dome and the Joseph Darlington Fountain at left there looms the D.C. Superior Court building at 500 Indiana Avenue. In other words, you can't get there from here anymore. Sadder, perhaps, is the embarrassing disrepair into which the fountain has descended. After years of neglect the fountain no longer works and its once-lovely pebble-lined pool has become a trash bin.

Surely she was always an oddity, this gilded callipygian nymph-cum-fawn on her marble pedestal fountain. In the first place, she looks nothing like Joseph Darlington, although certainly his 1876 portrait photographed in Brady's studio shows a fine-looking young fellow.

Some might have thought it strange that Joseph Darlington, a pillar of the Baptist church and a model of rectitude, would be honored with a statue of a pagan female nature spirit. Perhaps it was thought that neoclassical allusions tied the maiden in the foreground to the Capitol in the background. In any case, the nude and her pet fawn were not his decision. The statue was a posthumous salute from the deceased's admiring friends and fellow workers in the Washington Bar Association.

Joseph Darlington was born in 1849. At his death in 1920, he was "dean" of the Washington Bar, of which he was a member forty-six years. Darlington would have felt quite at home at the 5th and D Streets site of his memorial. After his graduation from Columbian Law School, then on 5th Street, he began practicing law with his young friends George E. Hamilton and John B. Larner at the 410 5th Street office of the Honorable Richard T. Merrick.

If you debark the D.C. Metro at Judiciary Square and walk to the Superior Court Building, the Darlington Memorial will stop you in your tracks. Mr. Darlington would probably have approved of the Metro; he disliked motor cars and refused to have them around. Satisfied clients tried to override his objections. A 1924 biographical sketch in the annals of the Columbia Historical Society noted, "After the Riggs Bank case, Mr. Charles C. Glover had delivered to his [Darlington's] home a fine, seven-passenger Packard limousine as a gift. Mr. Darlington and his family consented to go for a ride in Rock Creek Park in the car, but would not accept it, saying that he did not know anything about machinery." He similarly declined a limousine on another occasion.

His kindness, especially to the young and vulnerable, lived on in memory, creating a legacy that sometimes astonished his descendants. His granddaughter remembers that, growing up in Washington, she would sometimes be stopped in the street by people who would burst into tears as they recounted their memories of his goodness and generosity.

# U.S. CAPITOL

THIS somber view of the United States Capitol is another of the mysteriously ambiguous photographic compositions that Mr. Wentzel achieved by working on chill and foggy nights as airborne ice crystals diffused the light to astonishing effect. The complex geometry of the photograph might serve as a memorable illustration of that line from the quintessentially-1930s American poet, Edna St. Vincent Millay: "Euclid alone has looked on beauty bare."

The looming foreground shape is the fountain in front of Union Station, granite glinting in reflected light. It is one of a pair that flanks the Columbus fountain. The curve of this fountain and the shape of the Capitol dome, exploding in light, resonate harmoniously, the one an inversion of the other.

Capitol and capital both stem from the Latin word for head, *caput*. Before Washington, D.C.'s legislative building was an image recognized around the world, "capitol" was not the usual term for the seat of government, but was usually a reference to the Capitoline Hill, the smallest of ancient Rome's seven hills. Dome comes from the Latin word for house, *domus*, as in domestic and domicile; its French and Italian cousins, *dome* and *duomo*, both signify a cathedral. The silhouette of our capitol's dome suggests the domes of St. Paul's in London and St. Peter's in Rome. It particularly resembles St. Isaac's in St. Petersburg, the first iron dome ever constructed.

A German immigrant named August Schoenborn brought details of St. Isaac's when he came to work for the Philadelphia architect, Thomas Ustick Walter, who won the contest for a design to enlarge the Capitol. Walter's notebooks include St. Isaac's plans. It was Walter's idea to extend both the Capitol wings beneath the soaring (almost three hundred feet high) iron dome that has become our most familiar emblem. The copper-plated wooden dome that it replaced, (which looked more like an overturned teacup), had been the work of Boston architect Charles Bullfinch. He toiled from 1818 to 1826 to finish the Capitol. Within two decades, his version proved inadequate to house the burgeoning nation's legislators. With every new state more came.

Walter became the Capitol architect in 1851, chosen mostly for his work on Girard College in Philadelphia, in the 1830s the country's largest structure. The Girard project took Walter on a study trip to Europe from which he returned particularly impressed by the Pantheon built during the 18th century in Paris. In his Capitol work, Walters used more iron in the new House and Senate wings as well as the dome than in any previous American building; it came from a Brooklyn iron foundry called Janes, Beebe, and Kirtland. Contrary to popular legend, the Civil War never halted work on the dome; it was feared the iron would be pilfered if the project were neglected. (Work on the wings stopped in April 1861 but was resumed a year later because every rainstorm drenched the legislators.) By the end of 1863, the dome was finished.

# UNION STATION

SHIMMERING in the foggy night light here are the great doors to Union Station from which one can see the Capitol. Two rather stylish mid-30s figures in the middle distance have turned their back on the Capitol view, perhaps preferring to admire the south facade of white Vermont granite. Flanked by long arcaded wings, the monumental central loggia frames the doors in three arches among which stand massive Ionic columns. Above our line of sight, these columns support enormous allegorical sculptures by Louis Saint-Gaudens: Prometheus representing Fire, Thales (Electricity), Themis (Justice/Freedom/Knowledge), Apollo (Imagination), Ceres (Agriculture), and Archimedes (Mechanics). It is a good thing Saint-Gaudens was not assigned statues personifying micro-chips or nuclear fission.

Union Station was built during the 20th century's first decade, an expression of classic themes executed by Chicago architect Daniel H. Burnham in his capacity as director of works for the Columbian Exposition of 1893. Burnham's vision for Washington was focussed on this enormous structure, the first building to be completed under the impetus of the Park Commission. The cost of the project, which included reorganizing the city's scattered train tracks and several rail terminuses into one unified design with a 25-acre central facility, was borne by the federal government, the city, and the railroads involved. Alexander Cassatt, then president of the Pennsylvania Railroad, was the key player from the private sector. Congress passed the enabling legislation in 1903 and the building was completed in 1908.

Given the size and the sweep of the train station, these three great entrance doors were no more than adequate. Anything less in the way of an opening salvo would have been limp indeed. Inside the building one entered a main waiting room that measured 220 feet long and 120 feet wide. The great concourse that served the train shed was 760 feet long and 130 feet wide, a *Guiness Book of World Records* entry for unsupported sweep of roof and once the scene of the world's largest seated dinner. Much of the original interior space has been reorganized so that the quondam train station can function as a sort of spiffed-up shopping mall and entertainment center.

The train station of today seems tacked on the back as a sort of humble afterthought. But the front still looks the way it did when Mr. Wentzel photographed it in the mid-30s. You can still see that the point of this train station entrance was to impress the hoi polloi. Washington has been lucky to retain this colossal monument to the great age of transportation; such relics have in many cities been lost to neighborhood deterioration or the wrecking ball. And how fitting that our temple of transport should be on a sight line with our Capitol; for, surely, in numbering our national assets, transportation ranks right up there with political philosophy.

# SUPREME COURT

NIGHT lighting is best to look at the Supreme Court, for on a bright day, the white marble's gleam becomes an almost blinding glare. After they quarried the court's stone, there were probably too few marble chips left in the state of Vermont to grow a potful of paperwhites. The structure was brand new the night Mr. Wentzel took this photograph in 1935. The Supreme Court had just moved across the street from the Capitol, the physical manifestation of an emerging political truth.

Though much has been written of what our founding fathers drew from Montesquieu and *The Spirit of Laws*, about checks and balances, about the separation of political powers, the Constitution did not clearly forecast the importance of the Supreme Court. Limited expectations were reflected in city planning. When official buildings were constructed in Washington in the 1790s, a huge palace went up to house the Executive Branch and an even grander one for the Legislative Branch. The Judiciary had no place of its own to hang its periwig. The pomp and circumstance of red velvet curtains were far in the future; sometimes the court preferred to sit at nearby taverns, which were warmer and cozier than its uncomfortable quarters in the Capitol.

The court's growing importance was commensurate with the stature of its justices. The blazing white edifice to which the Court moved in the mid-30s was a marmoreal salute to William Howard Taft. Taft is the only American ever to hold the top posts in two of the three branches of government. He served as twenty-seventh president of the United States from 1909–1913, and in 1921, he became Chief Justice and served until 1930, resigning one month before his death. This post-White House position was unique in American history; few ex-presidents have gone back in harness. Andrew Johnson returned to Washington to serve in the Senate. After John Quincy Adams's four years as president, he served in the House of Representatives as a member from his native Massachusetts. He died in the Capitol after collapsing while addressing the House.

# JOHN MARSHALL

HOW FITTING that John Marshall contemplates the grounds of the Capitol, where the Supreme Court met during his years on the bench. When Mr. Wentzel photographed the statue in 1935, Marshall—appropriately—gazed from the west terrace toward the White House. As in life, he kept a sharp eye on "the President's Palace," and he never blinked. In any case, he no longer sits there. This statue was moved inside the Supreme Court and a copy of it was placed outside in Judiciary Square in 1984.

Born in Fauquier County, Virginia, in 1755, John Marshall served in the American Revolution, briefly studied law at William and Mary, and was called to the bar on what was then the western frontier. Elected a delegate to the Virginia assembly in 1782, he married and moved to Richmond, thenceforth his home. He served in all three branches of the government over a three-year period. He was elected to Congress as a Federalist in 1799. The next year, he became Secretary of State and in 1801 he was named Chief Justice.

Marshall led the court until his death in 1835, establishing its right to review the constitutionality of state and federal law. A loyal Federalist, he vastly expanded the central government's powers by his interpretation of the Constitution, which he held to be both a precise document and a living instrument of government.

The five-foot statue of Marshall is not his only brazen image on Capitol Hill. He also appears on the Supreme Court's 3,000-pound half-doors. Nearly twenty feet tall, the doors are decorated with bronze low-relief panels illustrating great moments in the history of the law: the Justinian Code; the signing of the Magna Carta; Lord Coke barring King James from the high court; and "Marshall and Story." In this last panel, sculptor John Donnelly shows John Marshall delivering the court's verdict in *Marbury* vs. *Madison*, the first in which an act of Congress was declared unconstitutional.

Joseph Story is depicted as a participant in this scene, but this is historically incorrect. Joseph Story was not on the court in 1803, at the time of *Marbury* vs. *Madison*; he served 1811–1845. Surely it was a cozy thought all the same, putting Story in a picture with Marshall, whose devoted adherent he was, considering that Justice Story was the father of William Wetmore Story, the Boston sculptor who created the statue of John Marshall that stands on the Capitol grounds seen here.

# LIBRARY OF CONGRESS

FROM watery paving of this plaza in front of the Library of Congress rises the ceremonial stair that leads to the bronze doors at the front entrance of what is now called the Jefferson Building. Flanking the three overarching doors are granite spandrels in which muse-like female figures are depicted. Above those is a balustrade, then a line of columns, behind which are five vast windows with broken pediments surmounted by busts of famous writers. At the top sits a collar-painted dome topped with a 23-carat gold leaf torch.

The inside is vastly more splendid, with towering ceilings, colonnades, mosaics, ornamental ironwork, frescoes, inlaid floors, stained glass, brown marble from Tennessee, yellow marble from Sienna, thirty-three keystone window ornaments sculpted with "savage and barbarous peoples" from the Smithsonian's ethnological collections, and much, much more.

In 1800, Congress's library was housed in the Capitol, and consisted of a few hundred books and nine maps. But it grew. In 1870, a revised copyright law demanded two copies of every U.S. publication for the Library of Congress. In they poured; soon there were roadblocks of books in the corridors of power.

The answer had to be a separate building for the books, but it was slow in coming. An architectural competition in 1873, won by John L. Smithmeyer and Paul J. Peltz, determined the design. Congress appropriated construction funds in 1886. In 1888, construction was supervised by the Army Chief of Engineers, Thomas Lincoln Casey, and in time his son who replaced Peltz. The building, which brought to mind the elaborate Beaux-Arts Paris Opera, was occupied in 1897.

A commemorative Wedgwood plate issued in 1900 featured an image of the Library of Congress inside a heavy ring of flowers. On the back of it was printed "It stands today the largest, most imposing, most sumptuous and most costly Library Building in the world."

Not everybody liked it. In 1898, Russell Sturgis, describing the flight of stairs seen here in Mr. Wentzel's photograph, complained of "that false idea of grandeur which consists mainly in hoisting a building up from a reasonable level off the ground, mainly in order to secure for it a monstrous flight of steps which must be surmounted before the main door can be reached . . . "

All the same, it made for a remarkable photographic composition.

The street lights probably aren't very efficient, either, but they certainly make an opulent statement. We wouldn't trade them for the world.

# NATIONAL ARCHIVES

MR. WENTZEL'S photograph sums up a lot about America's rich tradition. The foreground trees bespeak our natural resources, rich forests, fertile farmland, and rivers convenient for travel and water supply with falls to generate electric power. The car at left and neon, far right, suggest how we hitch our wagon not to a star but to the newest technological gimmicks: cotton gins, canals, steam engines, trains, telegraph, phones, planes, radio, television, microchips. Americans love new toys, demanding tomorrow's model today. When we see outmoded technology, we bow to its antiquity rather than what was once its potential. An old car? Quaint! We forget it was the harbinger of a new dawn.

The shimmering white Greco-Roman temple in the background reminds us that high political ideals "done built this city" in a new nation founded upon what was then perceived as classic precepts of democratic philosophy and republican ideals. The handful of people suggest that for all our numbers, we are a land of low population density with room for plenty more. These six people seem ready to cross Constitution Avenue to enter the place where they could view the Constitution itself.

The National Archives Building went where the old Center Market once stood. This market was also known as the "Marsh Market" because it was on such low ground. The Washington Canal used to carry Tiber Creek past this spot, with a wide turnaround basin into which fishmongers pitched offal. Captains were paid to drag dredges behind them to clear the channel so garbage could wash out of the sluggish canal. It did not work. "Boss" Shepherd's regime channelled it into pipes which were run under the street (then B Street, now Constitution Avenue.)

Until the National Archives Building was completed, just in time for Mr. Wentzel's 1935 photograph, the Library of Congress had charge of the precious documents of America's history; earlier, they had been in the State Department's library. These were surely wrenching changes. Similarly, the Army Corps of Engineers probably didn't turn handsprings when FDR reorganized the government in a way that took from them the task of showing city tourists their Washington heritage and handed over that lucrative patronage to the National Park Service. It was bad luck that when Franklin Delano Roosevelt took office, the Army Corps of Engineers' local operation was run by a man who gloried in the oh-so-Republican name of Ulysses S. Grant, III. Should a Grant be handing out all those fine federal jobs during a Democrat's administration?

As always in Washington, politics and change are a constant; the Archives continues to fulfill its destiny as the official repository of our national heritage, a role its dignified facade seems easily up to in this nighttime image.

# NATIONAL ARCHIVES

GUARDIANSHIP is an eight-foot limestone male figure, one of a pair flanking the Constitution Avenue entrance to the National Archives. Beneath it is the Jefferson quote, "Eternal vigilance is the Price of Liberty." The figure was wrought by James Earle Fraser, creator of more outdoor sculpture in Washington than anyone else.

A Minnesotan born in America's centennial year, Fraser studied at the Art Institute of Chicago and at Paris's Ecole des Beaux-Arts, working there and in New Hampshire as assistant to Augustus Saint-Gaudens. Fraser's best-known work is a coin, the "Buffalo" nickel, with the haunting "Iron Eyes" on the obverse. Another Fraser creation treating Native Americans is the well-known work *End of the Trail*.

At the National Archives, Fraser also sculpted the south pediment (deemed the city's finest), the acroterions, and medallions representing some departments of the federal government whose records were consigned to the archives: the Departments of Treasury, Interior, Commerce, War, and Navy.

The Supreme Court entrance is flanked by similar 1935 statues by Fraser. He created four pediments across the Department of Commerce facade, uneasy 1930s mesalliances between classical allusion and gritty modernism: *Aeronautics*'s nearly nude, muscle-bound heroes sport the aviation ace's leather cap. Fraser inscribed pithy sentiments beneath the four pediments, titled *Foreign and Domestic Commerce*, *Fisheries*, *Aeronautics*, and *Mining*: "The Patent System Added The Fuel of Interest To The Fire Of Genius: Lincoln," "Commerce Defies Every Wind—Outrides Every Tempest—And Invades Every Zone: Bancroft," "Commerce Among Nations Should Be Fair and Equitable: Franklin," and "Let Us Raise Standards To Which The Wise And Honest Can Repair: Washington."

Many of his works were integral parts of the buildings erected during the New Deal era, but Fraser also created free-standing monuments. His Second Division monument on the Ellipse is an 18-foot gilded bronze sword in a flaming aura that suggests a feather. He did the 1926 John Ericsson Monument ("He Revolutionized Navigation By His Invention Of The Screw Propeller") in West Potomac Park. For the Treasury, Fraser sculpted two early Secretaries, Alexander Hamilton, done in 1923, and Albert Gallatin, 1947.

His career spanned forty years, starting in 1911 with the Frederick Keep Monument in Rock Creek Cemetery and ending with his death two years after the 1951 installation of a pair of gilded equestrian statues on the circle at the Lincoln Memorial.

ETERNAL VIGILANCE
IS THE PRICE OF LIBERTY

# LABOR DEPARTMENT

I T IS A good thing Mr. Wentzel managed to get in to photograph the handsome stonework that ennobles the automobile access to the Labor Department, for this has subsequently become one of the city's less accessible spots. This photo seems to show us a magnificent carriage drive, and these buildings do not appear geared to the automotive age. Rather, they recall the "glory that was Greece, the grandeur that was Rome," and the elements of classical architecture that burst into flower in the Louvre-Tuileries complex, as noted in James Goode's introduction to this volume.

In his earlier book on outdoor sculpture in Washington, Mr. Goode points out that a number of neoclassical buildings in Paris were scrutinized by those charged with the execution of Federal Triangle structures and their decorations. Aesthetics were important, and one percent of the total budget was targeted for ornamentation of the buildings. Secretary of the Treasury Andrew Mellon, who would later be responsible for the nearby National Gallery of Art, played an important role in the development of the construction.

The huge complex of federal government buildings known as the Federal Triangle was, in a sense, spawned by the 1908 resolution of the American Historical Association, urging the legislative and executive branches to provide, in the nation's capital, a separate building in which government documents could successfully be preserved. Congress moved in 1913 to authorize the secretary of the treasury, then charged with the erection of government buildings, to produce plans for a fireproof national archive. Three years later, Congress moved on a public building program for a number of government buildings. The program depended heavily on the plans of the turn-of-the-century McMillan Commission's interpretation of L'Enfant's original design for the city, which called for structures to be erected in the neoclassical style favored by the city's 18th-century planners.

Although delayed by America's participation in World War I, the massive building scheme was heavily promoted in the 1920s by President Calvin Coolidge in his budget messages to the Hill. His recommendations became law in May 1926. Most of the job was completed between 1929 and 1938, but a portion of the work, behind the District Building, continues even as we go to print. Congress originally authorized the building of nine structures in the rhomboid bounded by 15th Streets and Pennsylvania and Constitution Avenues.

Wouldn't Federal Rhomboid be a curious name for a Metro stop?

# CORCORAN GALLERY OF ART

T HROUGH the balustrade on the west side of the State, War, and Navy Building (today's Old Executive Office Building) is the second Corcoran Gallery building (the collections moved in 1897 a couple of blocks from what is today known as the Renwick). This glorious expression of the City Beautiful leads a line of majestic non-governmental structures facing the Ellipse: headquarters buildings for the Red Cross, the Daughters of the American Revolution, and what was then the Pan American Union (now the Organization of American States).

Chartered by Congress in 1879, the Corcoran's goal was and is "the production and preservation of works pertaining to the fine arts, especially the work of our native painters and sculptors." A sampling from a mid-30s annual report of the Corcoran suggests its scope. Among works of art received as loans were Benjamin West's portrait of Stephen Carmick, P.A. deLazlo's portrait of John J. Pershing, and Jo Davidson's bronze bust of President Roosevelt. Works lent for exhibition included George Luks's *Woman with Black Cat*, Thomas Eakins's *Pathetic Song*, Seth Eastman's *Ball Playing Among the Sioux Indians*, Childe Hassam's *Old House at Easthampton*, and *The Long Story* by William S. Mount. Mr. Julius Garfinckel lent etchings by James A. McNeill Whistler for an exhibit. Nine oil paintings were purchased, including *Monadnock* by Abbott H. Thayer and *Adirondacks* by Rockwell Kent.

Heartening crowds viewed the art. With 428 paintings by 35 artists, the March 1935 exhibition was attended by 6,229 persons, "nearly twice the number who attended the opening of the 13th Biennial." The director was pleased by the increased use of artistic facilities, with 312 students in the art school, 37 more than in 1933. "The studio for visiting artists provided in the Gallery has been in frequent use. Mr. Jo Davidson worked for some time on a sculptural project for the Tennessee Valley Dam." He also was concerned with the fabric of the building. "The Potomac Electric Power Co. has notified the Gallery that, about July 1st, they will change the electric service which they furnish from direct current to alternating current." And then there was heat. The gallery benefitted from a provision in H.R. 9830 that "The Treasury Department is authorized to furnish heat from this plant to the Corcoran Gallery of Art."

Elsewhere in the 1935 Corcoran report, it was noted, "as the Trustees know, the health of Mr. Glover, Sr., the President Emeritus of our Board and its oldest member, remains unchanged. Throughout the years during which he has been confined to his home by illness his absence from our meetings has been keenly felt."

# N.Y. AVE. PRESBYTERIAN CHURCH

THIS CHURCH, where Lincoln had once prayed, was demolished in 1950 and rebuilt on the same spot. The new structure was similar to the earlier one, but extended further back toward 14th Street. Dr. Peter Marshall's sermons drew crowds; eventually it was necessary to double the church's floor space. A search committee of Judge Whitaker of the Court of Claims and A. Chambers Oliphant had lured the Scots-born pastor up from Atlanta in the late 30s when his predecessor, Dr. Sizoo, had been called to the Fifth Avenue Presbyterian Church in New York. Sizoo, too, had sermonized with a distinctive burr. His curious way of pronouncing "world" as "wortle" baffled the young.

Peter Marshall built on previous decades of success. Earlier in the 20th century, the men's Bible class was one of *the* places to see and be seen. During the Civil War era the Lincoln family walked two blocks from the White House for services. The president came also of an evening to pray there. Mary Lincoln obviously had a cordial relationship with the wife of the pastor, Phineas D. Gurley, and on May 19, 1862, wrote:

> "My Dear Mrs. Gurley,
>   Our consul at Smyrna sent me a few boxes of figs. I take the liberty
>   of sending you a taste of raisins & figs, a little different from those we
>   get here. Hoping your daughter's health is improving, I remain truly
>   —Mary Lincoln"

Lincoln's growing renown made the church a hallowed shrine, a "must see" on many sightseeing lists. In 1929, what had once been the city's tallest steeple (blown down in an 1896 windstorm) was replaced through the philanthropy of Mrs. Robert Todd Lincoln, widow of the firstborn son of "the martyred president." Stabilizing the new steeple meant sinking a base down in the basement, displacing organ pipes.

Lincoln's revered place in American hearts and Marshall's magnetism in the pulpit packed the old church. The choir and the congregation's overflow were perched up on precarious little balconies. The fire marshall worried.

Architect Edward Haviland had designed the 1859 colonial revival building, one of the city's first in that style, embellished with some curious Italian design elements. This oddity was demolished, preservation having few proponents in 1950.

Ironically, after the flight to the suburbs during the 1960s, Haviland's original structure would have been ample for the Presbyterians who were still around.

# WASHINGTON CIRCLE

IN THE 1930s, Works Progress Administration Federal Writers' Project city guide to the nation's capital wrote "Washington Circle, at the joint intersection of Pennsylvania and New Hampshire Avenues with K and Twenty-third Streets, is one of the most attractive of the city's smaller 'breathing areas.'"

Columbia Hospital has long stood in the neighborhood. At the time of this photograph, George Washington University Hospital was still on H Street near 14th; when it moved to Washington Circle, this became the city's premier medical area. In spite of ambulances streaming toward the circle, screaming through the night, the residential quality remained.

Even today, a surprising amount of low-density housing radiates out toward Foggy Bottom and Dupont Circle. Bookshops and cafés teem with George Washington University students. Until very recently, a jeweler would fix your watch. You could buy a drink from a bartender who knew your name, pawn your tiara, see an offbeat film, buy an apple at a Mom-and-Pop store. At drug store soda fountains, pretty matrons rehashed their analytic "hours."

Amid eye-catching whirls of outbound traffic this photograph shows Clark Mills's 1860 equestrian statue of George Washington. The enthusiastic response to Mills's 1850 statue of Andrew Jackson prompted this commission, but his earlier success was not repeated. Mills modelled a stony-faced Washington from the famous Houdon bust, but the phlegmatic phiz seemed all wrong. There was a public outcry against this incongruity—the composed George Washington astride a steed with rolling eyeballs, flared nostrils, neck arched in terror.

You could, nevertheless, claim that in this equestrian statue, "its sculptor well those passions read," for, all his life, George Washington was famed for his calmness in the face of fire as well as his accomplished seat on a horse.

His horses did not have that same track record. More than one was shot out from under him in the 1755 rout at Fort Duquesne, which battle brought young Washington international fame. His credentials as commander-in-chief of the Virginia Militia were deemed insufficient and he was denied a commission in the British Army; still, he went with General Edward Braddock from Alexandria through Foggy Bottom, up today's Wisconsin Avenue, northwest to near the present site of Pittsburgh. Braddock was ambushed and killed, as were many other British officers. The quick-witted young Washington concealed Braddock's corpse lest the French and Indians learn the troops were leaderless. Indeed they were not, for the young Virginian led the survivors to safety. His name became a household word.

# SCOTT CIRCLE

THIS peaceful snow scene featuring the bronze equestrian statue of General Winfield Scott shows us his circle looking far calmer than it ever would again. Even back in 1937, the W.P.A. Guide stated that "At the joint intersection of Massachusetts and Rhode Island Avenues with Sixteenth and N Streets . . . with its inner and outer rings of surging traffic, this is for pedestrians probably the most hazardous ground within the District."

And it's not just traffic that's confusing. On the east side of Scott Circle is the Hahnemann Memorial exedra and on the opposite side stands a statue of Daniel Webster. Talk about the jumble stop approach.

Scott is a lot easier to memorialize in this photograph than at the actual site. And certainly he deserves to be remembered. Scott served longer at a higher rank than any other U.S. military figure.

Winfield Scott was born near Petersburg, Virginia in 1786 and was educated as a lawyer. Going from the militia into the regular army, he made a name for himself in the War of 1812 at Queenstown Heights (1812), Chippewa and Lundy's Lane (1814). By war's end he had been captured, exchanged, and finally brevetted major general.

Scott was sent to Europe to study military tactics and act as a government agent. In the course of a long and varied career, he wrote the first standard set of American military drill regulations. In 1832, he fought in the Black Hawk War and also participated in quieting nullification troubles. He supervised the removal of the Cherokees to Indian Territory in 1838, having also been involved in campaigns to subdue the Seminole and Creek. The next year he was involved in settling the Aroostook War over the boundary between Maine and New Brunswick.

The Mexican War (1846–1848) brought Scott such fame that he was nominated for the presidency. Unfortunately for Scott, he was invited to run on the ticket of the disintegrating Whig party and he lost to Franklin Pierce's landslide vote. In spite of the loss, his military service continued and he went to Washington Territory in 1859 to settle the San Juan Boundary Dispute.

Winfield Scott exemplifies the Southern military man who never questioned his allegiance to the Union. He opposed secession and was a loyal Unionist. As commander-in-chief at the outbreak of the Civil War his sentiments were unwavering, but while the spirit was willing the flesh was weak. By then, he was derisively nicknamed Old Fuss 'n' Feathers, an unkind reference to his geriatric maundering and his outmoded ideas of glorious military trappings. Having served every president since Thomas Jefferson, Scott sent Lincoln his request for retirement in the autumn of 1861; the president and his cabinet met next day at the old soldier's home to eulogize his career. Scott died at West Point in 1866.

# HAHNEMANN STATUE

DR. SAMUEL Hahnemann, the father of homeopathy, is framed in the sparkle of ice-glittered trees as he contemplates a crescent of snow. The reverence accorded by Mr. Wentzel's Speed Graphic echoed what was once near-universal acclaim for this trail-blazing German physician. Hahnemann (1755–1843) was practicing medicine in Leipzig when he came up with "Similia Similibus Curentur," the "law of similars" based on the curative powers of drugs that induced the symptoms of a given disease when dispensed to healthy people. His theories gained wide acceptance. He was skilled in dispensing appropriate doses at a time when over-medication was the more general practice. Most of his success, however, stemmed from being the best of a bad lot—the practice of medicine was in its infancy—but if Hahnemann's reasoning was faulty, at least his ideas were executed with compassion and talent.

Mr. Wentzel remembers shooting this picture because he liked the scene, indeed, a handsome one. The life-sized bronze Hahnemann, stands on the east side of Scott Circle, Massachusetts Avenue at 16th Street. Beneath a dome of striking mosaic, Hahnemann is flanked by four bronze relief panels showing him as student and chemist, teacher and doctor, all in the form of a Greek exedra, a curving bench. Mr. Wentzel may have been prompted to photograph Hahnemann on account of their shared German birth. The Wentzel family left Dresden for upper New York state in 1926, when he was still a schoolchild.

Germans seeking Teutonic mementos find little in the nation's capital. There's Martin Luther, two blocks distance from Hahnemann on Thomas Circle. Frederick the Great stood at the war college until 1946. Though the German community in Washington was small, it was represented on the boards of local banks in disproportionately high percentages. Germans in Washington have, over the decades, had their own social clubs, charities, cemeteries, churches, and schools, some of them having survived more than a century.

It is curious that the Germanic heritage has left us with so little evidence of its strength. Second only to the British isles, Germany is the source of more of our ancestors here in the United States than any other land. Until quite recent times, German came right after English as our most-spoken tongue. But people here seem to pass by all this unawares, just as they do the Hahnemann statue.

# DANIEL WEBSTER STATUE

A GHOSTLY aureole of light outlines the statue of Daniel Webster, who looks toward the equestrian statue of Lieutenant General Winfield Scott, in his Circle, at 16th Street and Massachusetts Avenue. Darkness and shrubbery obscure the bronze panel at the base of the statue's back and its inscription, "Our country, our whole country and nothing but our country." These ringing, if derivative, words were from Daniel Webster's dedication of the Bunker Hill Monument, honoring the first major military engagement of the American Revolution (actually, at nearby Breed's Hill on June 17, 1775). Webster's skill as a public speaker won him great fame, his gifts acknowledged by friends and foes alike.

Washington diarist Benjamin Brown French was fascinated by news of Webster's oration, but his private journal entry about the dedication shows his own subjective view. In 1847 Brown became president of the Magnetic Telegraph Company: what strikes Brown as remarkable was the speed with which he could read about the dedication—nary a word of Webster's stirring address. Here are French's observations of what's depicted on the bronze panel.

"Monday, June 19. [1843] As evidence of the astonishing rapidity with which information is now spread over this land, I record here that I, this morning, at 9 o'clock read at the Capitol a large portion of Mr. Webster's speech delivered at the Bunker Hill celebration in Boston on Saturday last, probably about noon! It was in this city between 4 & 5 o'clock this morning. Thus, in less than 40 hours, from the time of delivery, we have a speech written out, printed & distributed more than 4 hundred miles from the place of delivery & all by the ordinary mail intercourse! Could the speech have left Boston instantly on its delivery and travelled at the rate of 10 miles an hour, it could not have reached here at the time it did. Then, when we deduct the time required to write it out from the rough notes of the Stenographer, the delay in printing it in New York (for it was the N.Y. *Herald* edition that I read) the time required to fold, pack, & direct the papers, we may form some idea of the speed at which it travelled! What's the use of speculating about balloons, when information can pass from one end of the Union to the other at the rate of 20 miles an hour! But, astonishing as this is, only a few years will elapse when, by the aid of electromagnetism, miles will be converted into inches, & hours into seconds; the thought that occurs in the *heart* here in Washington, will be instantly known to all the acknowledged of this widespread Union! As the poor Irish woman said, upon some new invention being explained to her, 'What a beautiful world this will be *when it is finished* . . . '"

# DUPONT CIRCLE

IN THE 1880s, city maps called this spot Pacific Circle not because of any watery associations but because it was the city's residential Far West. The area began to go "uptown" when William Morris Stewart, the mining millionaire Senator from Nevada, raised a turreted "castle" on the circle in 1875. In 1884, a portrait statue of Rear Admiral Samuel Francis duPont (1803–1865) was placed in this circle as well. This honor righted the wrong done when he was relieved of his command after failing to take Charleston by sea. Secretary of the Navy Gideon Welles had insisted on the attack, believing that the new monitors (iron gunboats) were impregnable. Dupont's forces were turned back by an enormous volume of shot from Forts Sumter and Moultrie.

In time, Dupont Circle was ringed with some of the city's most substantial residences, lavishly equipped to vie with each other in dispensing hospitality through the Washington "season" that ran from the Supreme Court's October opening until Lent. These in-town chateaux and palazzi rose on comparatively small wedges of land, though there might be space outside for a dog run or a "terrapin moat" in which would sulk the wherewithal for such delicacies as "Lady Curzon Soup." Daughters of the neighborhood were among the "dollar princesses" who married titled Europeans.

Different hostesses had different nights to give their weekly "germans," a dancing evening characterized by party favors distributed after each dance set. When the season ended, you could go abroad in search of more beads, fans, parasols, and combs to give away at next year's parties.

Admiral duPont's family took him home to Wilmington, where his statue stands in Rockford Park; they commissioned Daniel Chester French to design the fountain installed in 1921. Henry Bacon was the architect. The large white marble works harmoniously with the width of the circle. Its classical style is particularly appropriate to the house Stamford White designed for the Robert Wilson Pattersons at 15 Dupont Circle.

The fountain's wide, graceful basin catches the upper bowl's overflow. The stem is a wide column of three allegorical figures in graceful classical drape. Their symbols suggest the arts of ocean navigation. A woman who holds a boat in one hand, stroking a gull with the other, symbolizes the sea. The stars are represented by a female figure holding a globe. The wind is the male figure Mr. Wentzel photographed in 1936, draped in the wind-filled sail of a ship, holding a conch shell horn.

The two women-one male ratio somehow suggests Dupont Circle's goings on during the high stepping era between the Wars: the men were somewhat less noticed than the ladies, who gave every evidence of relishing the social ramble.

# QUE STREET BRIDGE

P EOPLE once called this area the West End because the capital stopped at Rock Creek. Beyond the city of Washington, Georgetown, with its own separate street system, had been a thriving tobacco port since the mid-18th century, well before there was either a nation's capital or a nation.

Washington was first linked to Georgetown by a bridge near the mouth of the Creek. By the mid-19th century, there was a bridge at P Street, beside the ruins of the paper mill. The "million dollar" Taft Bridge has spanned the Creek at Connecticut Avenue since 1911.

Dumbarton Bridge, also known as Que Street Bridge, was built in 1914. Its photograph is a rewarding study for many reasons, not least of which is the difficulty of scrutinizing the bridge, as we usually do, from the disadvantageous view from a car. Even this nighttime view of the Turkish Embassy, upper right, and the bridge in the center shows more than most motorists see as they speed along Rock Creek Parkway.

There is, for example, the 12-degree horizontal curve whereby the bridge accommodates the slight change of direction in Que Street. Before the bridge was built, Que didn't get past 23rd Street in Washington. What we now think of as its extension in Georgetown was then a Stoddert Street cul-de-sac. A handsome brick house called Bellevue blocked access to the Creek. As plans for this bridge came to fruition, the house was an impediment. One white horse was hitched up to swing the house out of progress' path and, little by little, day by day, the house was moved to its present location at 2715 Que Street. With Fiske Kimball as its champion and Horace Peaslee as hands-on architect, the house was acquired in 1928 by the National Society of Colonial Dames of America and became their national headquarters. Since that time it has been called Dumbarton House, a tribute to the name on the original land patent: Ninian Beall, who named his tract "Rock of Dumbarton."

The bridge is usually called the Que Street Bridge or the Buffalo Bridge for its four American bison, the work of sculptor A. Phimister Proctor. You might expect some nickname would recall the twenty-eight Indian heads on each side of the bridge. But no.

The bridge has five arch spans suggesting the construction of a Roman aqueduct. It was designed by Washington architect Glenn Brown and his son Bedford. As secretary of the McMillan Commission during the first quarter of the century, Glenn Brown played a notable role in turn-of-the-century city planning here. He persuaded the American Institute of Architects to move here from New York, and to acquire and save the Octagon for its headquarters.

# HENDERSON CASTLE

THIS enormous Romanesque pile stood on 16 Street, across from the foot of Meridian Hill Park. "Henderson's Castle" was razed in 1949; a townhouse development went up there in 1976. The Hendersons were rich in worldly goods and even richer in biographical material. John Brooks Henderson, born in 1826, was the Missouri Senator who drafted the Thirteenth Amendment, the Constitutional amendment that abolished slavery. His death in 1913 prompted his teetotal widow to smash all his liquor bottles, the very opposite of a wake.

A law unto herself, Mary Foote Henderson was viewed as an entrepreneurial social queen who developed "her" street into what in 1913 was grandly (if briefly) christened "Avenue of the Presidents." With "her" architect George Oakley Totten, she developed a dozen of the city's most opulent mansions in the area a few blocks north of her house. Most became embassies. When built in 1888, her house was called "Boundary Castle," rising as it did on 16th Street at Florida Avenue, originally Boundary because it marked the end of the City of Washington within the District (or Territory) of Columbia.

What would deepen the power of this dramatic photograph would have been headlines about the scandal that engulfed Mrs. Henderson's last days. To keep her estate intact, the granddaughter had tried to put Grannie away but Mrs. Henderson countered with testimony that the young woman was not the genuine article. The inference was that, on the day she was born, Mrs. Henderson's son and his wife banished their usual retinue of servants from an isolated country retreat. A nurse from a nearby country doctor's office recounted rumors of an infant impostor, smuggled into the Henderson menage. It was said that the daughter-in-law stopped stuffing her skirt top with pillows, ending the pseudocyesis farce, and the son presented the formidable Mrs. Henderson with the longed-for grandchild heiress. Who was this young person to decide whether Mrs. Henderson should leave her castle as a residence for the Vice President?

When Mrs. Henderson died, aged ninety in 1931, her will benefitted her Japanese secretary who later made an out-of-court settlement giving the adopted granddaughter most of the estate. Ah, but the jewels! Where had they gone? Did Mrs. Henderson squirrel them away in the house? All its contents went on the block in 1935 and boarders lived there from 1937 until the house was demolished.

Did some lucky auction-goers bring home a credenza with a false-bottom drawer jammed with pearls? Did one of the lodgers press a secret panel revealing parures and tiaras? Did the wrecking ball lay open a cache of diamonds?

And had you found it, would you have told?

# DOORMAN AT THE TROIKA

THE TROIKA was a downtown Washington night spot drenched in the romance of refugees and the doomed world of White Russians who fled the Soviet Union after the Russian Revolution at the end of World War I. These decorative but unskilled aristocrats survived by selling off their jewelry, making a meager living churning out memoirs and millinery, or so it was fondly believed. Legend held that in Paris they drove taxis and in New York they ran restaurants. Washington had a rather spare Russian community—a few translators and bibliophiles at the Library of Congress, a small Russian Orthodox congregation that met in a private house, some diplomats from the old days who had married Americans.

Even back in the 1850s, the Russian ministers had an eye for pretty local girls. The Baron de Bodisco married Harriet Miller, a Georgetown schoolgirl of modest background; the Russian Court viewed this union as a morganatic marriage. Later, Count George Bakhmeteff married Marie Beale.

The Russian emigre conjured up a nostalgic image that appealed to Washingtonians. To capitalize on this pleasant melancholy, the doorman dressed in Old World attire. His veiled, far-away gaze might give customers a little *frisson* of anxiety, followed by an inner sigh of relief that it didn't happen here. Blood ran in the streets of Moscow, not Washington.

The Troika was at 1011 Connecticut Avenue north of Farragut Square. Its name meant the Russian vehicle drawn by three horses abreast, a word known to all who grew up hearing the McGuffey reader kind of fable about the Russian family fleeing a wolf pack. The word *troika* has mournful associations for many.

The film *Roberta* evoked La Vielle Russie, as did tunes like "Smoke Gets In Your Eyes," the haunting strains of the balalaika, the tang of borscht, evocative genre paintings, and the dizzying wallop of vodka, which everyone believed to be made of potatoes. It felt good to feel so bad. The customers could be transported back to a magical land they had never known. The next time they picked up the society pages, they would feel at one with the likes of Serge Obelensky, even Mike Romanoff.

So the Troika's doorman and his sorrowful countenance were part and parcel of the experience. He might be looking away in response to a wrenching memory of vanished glory. On the other hand, he might be looking down Connecticut Avenue to call you a cab.

# THE WATERFRONT

ONE of the delights of dining in the shadow of the Washington Monument is the available seafood. Early explorers claimed they found so many sturgeon they could cross the Potomac walking across their backs. Buyboats traversed "the great protein factory" called the Chesapeake Bay, collecting fish from bugeyes and skipjacks. Sent to fetch big city prices, boats that sold the catch jammed the Washington Channel during the mid-1930s when Mr. Wentzel caught this dramatic shot. Between Maine Avenue and the river's edge, raw bars and restaurants offered warm-weather food service on upstairs porches and balconies. Diners caught breezes off the river, viewed Virginia (they might even see planes take off from the Washington-Hoover Airport at the west end of the 14th Street Bridge), and threw pennies down to tap dancing children. Before Southwest urban redevelopment swept out much of the resident population, the waterfront teemed with youngsters.

The fishmonger might be a tenth-generation waterman, his speech tinged with Elizabethan English, with a family back home on some remote Bay island that never had a resident physician. The buyer might be a proud hostess looking for a dozen perfectly matched pairs of shad roe to appear on a silver platter ringed with lemon halves clad daintily in cheesecloth to keep their seeds out of the fish eggs. Church groups bought bushels of blues for their Sunday night crab boil. In spring, customers in the know sought out rockfish livers, engorged for the fish's arduous mating season; this was believed a healthful food, like the "liver and lights" of the cod which translated into the 1930s' despised childhood nutrition supplement of codliver oil. A family would get a barrel of oysters in the fall and keep it out in the garage under damp gunny sacks, feeding the oysters an occasional fistful of cornmeal. As long as the shells were shut fast, the oysters were alive and edible; an open shell meant the muscle had relaxed because the oyster was dead. A really fresh oyster on the half shell should wince when the lemon juice hits it, or so old oystermen claimed.

Eastern Shore men would get you a good terrapin; they kept long poles handy with hooks on the end to flip over the carapace and immobilize the prey for capture. When they took your money, they'd give you a tall tale with your change: all four limbs of the terrapin taste differently—one like venison, another like possum meat, another like chicken, another like beef—because God assembled the terrapin out of leftover parts when He had finished creating the other, more homogenized animals.

# WASHINGTON MONUMENT

THE Washington Monument gleams brightly in Mr. Wentzel's mid-1930s night view, having been cleaned for the first time the previous year by the Works Progress Administration. It was almost a two-year task to erect the tubular steel scaffolding encasing the shaft. The actual scrub-down of the monument, achieved by a vigorous steel brush abrasion with sand-and-water, took less than five months. While the scaffolding was up, a thief made off with the platinum-tipped lightning conductors surrounding the 100-ounce aluminum pyramid that tops the monument.

It was even bigger news when Walter Johnson, pitcher for the Washington Senators, tossed a ball from the top.

Security must have been lax when "The Big Train" threw the ball out the Monument window. Prior to the 1970s, the public had free access to the whole interior of the Monument. Ascending the 898 steps was a rite of passage for Washington children, an expedition frequently undertaken to mark a significant birthday. "How many times have you done the Monument stairs?" was a frequent childhood query. And even more important, "Up? Or down?"

The Monument's first elevator was a steam hoist. In 1900, this was replaced by an electric elevator, which took five minutes to reach the top. In 1927, a new elevator made the trip in one and one quarter minutes. You can still ascend fast, but you can no longer take the leisurely "excelsior" hike. The stairs have been closed, for patrolling them is too difficult.

The shaft's interior was a spell-binding place to loiter, a treasure trove of strange phenomena and unlikely souvenirs. When very warm weather comes on fast after a cold spell, it "rains" inside the Monument due to condensation of the atmosphere within the shaft because of the relatively slow response of the stone walls to outside changes of temperature. Regardless of the weather, the Monument's interior is a singular vertical history lesson, lined as it is with more than two hundred stones from individual citizens, from cities and counties, from states and territories, and from abroad.

Many have enlightening inscriptions. The stone from New Bedford, Massachusetts, has a lapidary whale to denote the industry that made the town rich. California proclaims itself "the youngest sister of the Union;" Utah used the name "Deseret" on its stone. A stone from the Cherokee Nation honored the first "Great White Father." From Rome, the Pope sent a marble block from the Temple of Concord in 1854, which inflamed the anti-Catholic sentiments of the "American Party." "Know Nothing" hoodlums heaved it into the Potomac and managed to vote themselves in charge of the Monument Society. Their clumsy maneuvers checked the Monument's rise at about a third of its eventual 555-foot height. To this day, it is easy to see where construction halted. Army engineers finished the building. The world's tallest masonry structure was dedicated in 1884.

# LINCOLN MEMORIAL

IN THIS night view of the Lincoln Memorial echoed in the 2,000 foot-long reflecting pool, Mr. Wentzel's camera has made an abstraction from the architecture and sculpture of realism. The statue of Lincoln looks as much like Honest Abe as the "Dean of American sculptors," Daniel Chester French, could manage. The structure itself is the most authentic classical temple that architect Henry Bacon could achieve.

But the result, as Mr. Wentzel captured it, is more inference than representation, and the light is what makes the difference. In H.P. Caemmerer's 1932 *magnum opus*, *Washington/The National Capital*, he explains "The interior is lighted through translucent panels of marble and by the great front opening. Recently a special system of lighting was installed."

The 1937 W.P.A. Guide notes: "Throughout the interior, the floors and the wall base are of pink Tennessee marble. Walls are of Indiana limestone, and the ceiling is of thin marble panels supported by a framework of bronze girders. These panels are treated in the old Florentine manner with a saturation of beeswax to make them translucent. The daylight reaching the inner hall through the eastern opening is supplemented and softened by the quieter glow diffused through the marble ceiling." Sounds like a fairly straightforward situation. The daylight came down through a translucent marble ceiling. Ah, but wait.

The precedent was that when marble was properly oiled, light could stream through it. But when the Lincoln Memorial was complete in 1926, the ceiling seemed dingy, the light definitely clouded. The Army Engineers decided on drastic action. If a "saturation of beeswax in the old Florentine manner" had not admitted enough light, they would move on to heavy duty, industrial strength grease.

According to a kinsman of the officer in charge, one night in June 1930, a platoon of volunteers wearing waders was sent atop the Lincoln Memorial. This was done *sub rosa*. Reverence for the Great Emancipator, then at its very height, demanded decorum. On the roof, they used long-handled brooms to scrub bucketloads of lard into the marble slabs to heighten their light-transmitting powers.

Throughout the summer, the Engineers checked anxiously on the translucency of the richly anointed ceiling. There was no appreciable gain in illumination. It seemed that though oiling Italian marble might bring the sun's beams streaming through it, the domestic stuff remained obdurately opaque. And it smelled. In the blazing heat of July noons, the discerning nose caught whiffs of melting pig fat. This exercise in bringing home the bacon was called a failure and, come September, they donned their waders again, went back up on the roof, and in secrecy scrubbed away the lard.

# LINCOLN MEMORIAL

ABOUT the seated Lincoln enshrined in the Lincoln Memorial, the sculptor himself noted "The memorial tells you just what manner of man you are come to pay homage to; his simplicity, his grandeur and his power."

It seems likely that whole monographs could be penned on just the degree of tension in Lincoln's left hand. This photograph presents it as not precisely a clenched fist, but no limp-wristed appendage, either. These are not idle fingers. We see here the hand of a backwoods log-splitter and, when he had to be, a nation splitter, in the views of some critics.

Washingtonians can ponder the thoughts inspired by this work of art at their leisure, but not as it's seen here; Mr. Wentzel's photograph offers a rare look at the drama of the statue at night. It's obvious why such an effort was made to get the lighting just right, for illumination is the key to the experience of seeing this most famous of all works by any American sculptor.

The man who did the job was Daniel Chester French (1850–1931), well born, gifted, and well rewarded for his artistic achievements, which range from the 1875 *Minute Man* in Concord, Massachusetts, to the fountain at the center of Dupont Circle. Although his New England studio at *Chesterwood* is the place most associated with French, he is well represented in the nation's capital, and never more impressively than by his seated Lincoln. The figure is almost twenty feet tall, the flag-draped chair a dozen feet high. Of crystalline Georgia marble, the statue is twenty blocks of stone fitted together seamlessly. The New York stonecutting firm of Piccarilli spent four years executing the job.

Lincoln looks out from under his craggy brow, up toward the Capitol; his Memorial, begun in 1915 and dedicated in 1922, seems to mark the end of the Mall just as naturally as the Capitol begins it. In 1791, when he first spotted the site where he put the capitol, our city's designer Pierre L'Enfant was enthusiastic about "erecting the Federal House [at] the western end of Jenkin's Heights [which] stands ready as a pedestal waiting for a superstructure & I am confident were all the ground cleared of wood, no other situation could bear competition with this." In other words, Capitol Hill was a natural. And to most of us alive today, the Lincoln Memorial seems the Mall's inescapable conclusion.

Prior to World War I, however, the Mall as we know it was not a given and there was heated debate about stretching the city's monumental core towards the Potomac. Foggy Bottom was an area of gasworks and lowlife, on low-lying land reclaimed from the Potomac River's tidal flats. When confronted with the McMillan Commission's plan to set the Lincoln Memorial at the foot of the Mall, "Uncle Joe" Cannon, speaker of the House, insisted that "I'll never let a memorial to Abraham Lincoln be erected in that God-damned swamp." Well, Cannon misfired. The Memorial went up, Lincoln went in. The whole thing is one of the wonders of the world.

# WASHINGTON MONUMENT

IF heroes' monuments indicate their fame and popularity, let it be noted that in 1783, six years before he was elected president, Congress decreed "that an equestrian statue of General Washington be erected at the place where Congress shall be established . . . in honor of . . . the illustrious Commander in Chief of the Armies of the United States of America during the War which vindicated and secured their liberty, sovereignty, and independence."

George Washington on horseback would bespeak the commander in chief as a model of republican Roman virtue, in contrast to America's only previous equestrian statue (of George III), famous for having been pulled down by a New York mob in 1776.

There had been abundant effort to honor the first president in marble and bronze. John Marshall proposed a marble tomb shortly after Washington died. This proposal won Martha Washington's consent but the Senate failed to pass the appropriation. During the two-year wrangle over money, his widow, too, was buried at Mount Vernon.

As the 19th century moved along, mourning escalated to hagiographic frenzy. Schoolgirls stitched weeping willows. Washington's Tomb was a lithographic favorite. In 1816, the General Assembly of Virginia tried to reinter Washington in suitable splendor in Richmond. Governor Wilson Cary Nicholas could not wrestle the first president's bones away from his nephew Bushrod Washington, an associate Supreme Court Justice who kept the remains at Mount Vernon where he then lived.

In 1819, Senator Goldsborough of Maryland introduced a bill to memorialize Washington, as, in 1824, did Representative James Buchanan of Pennsylvania. During his first year as president, John Quincy Adams tried for a suitable monument but failed; so did Henry Clay's effort in the centennial year of Washington's birth, 1832.

Decisive action was instigated by George Watterston, formerly Librarian of Congress: in 1833, the Washington National Monument Society met to elect Chief Justice Marshall its first president. He was succeeded by presidents serving *ex officio*. (You can get a lot done in this city if you don't care who gets the credit.)

Every American was urged to contribute one dollar; later, the Washington Monument Society accepted larger amounts.

The final result looks glorious as Mr. Wentzel photographed it through the columns of the Lincoln Memorial. But it certainly is a long way from George Washington on a horse as Congress ordered in 1783.

# THE MALL

**H**ERE BY NIGHT is perhaps the city's most classic view, the Capitol dome behind the shaft of the Washington Monument viewed through the Lincoln Memorial's fluted Doric columns. The concept seems to have been cast in stone. By George, it *was* cast in stone. Could the nation's capital have possibly looked any other way?

Actually it was meant to. Major Pierre Charles L'Enfant, George Washington's Engineering Corps protege, planned the City of Washington with an east-west axis running from the Capitol to the river. On the Mall (which he planned as an embassy-lined, bustling pedestrian thoroughfare, not a sylvan retreat), this line would cross the meridian, (the north-south of 16th Street) through the White House. Where these lines intersected, L'Enfant would dip the knee to his benefactor: an equestrian statue of General Washington would arise.

It did not. L'Enfant lost the power to make it happen. His aesthetic vision, though inspired, was crippled by the artist's arrogance. Less than a year into his grand city design, he was brought low by the city commissioners, politicians, and property-holders. Though his city plan was, in the main, adhered to, he was fired and died penniless and disgraced.

Decades passed without a monument to Washington arising. Finally a private group, the Washington Monument Society, called for designs. Architectural competitions were a thrifty source of building plans (the risk was in the designer's court). The 1836 competition was won by the eminent South Carolinian architect Robert Mills, already responsible for the nation's first major monument to George Washington, the 165-foot column in Baltimore. It was Mills's view that "monuments have always served as beacons of safety to public virtue and beacons of warning to the vicious."

Mills called for a 700-foot shaft with a 100-foot-tall circular temple at its base, ringed with Doric columns and topped with classical statuary. Over the entrance would be a quadriga like the one atop Berlin's Brandenburg Gate. Mills's winning entry seems to recall such notable antique sources as Hadrian's Tomb (Tosca's jumping off point, the Castel Sant' Angelo) and the Mausoleum of Halicarnassus as Mills would have known it (or at least, pictures of it) in the Comte de Caylus's 1759 reconstruction, an obelisk atop a colonnaded base mixing "*les formes Egyptiennes & l'elegance des ornemans Grecs.*" Though the Washington Monument rose only 555 feet without Mills's planned temple base, the diminished obelisk was still too heavy for the site where L'Enfant's two axes intersected. And so the shaft rose a hundred yards to the southeast on higher, firmer ground. To our eyes, it seems to have belonged there from the start.

The mysterious seated figure who seems to perfectly define the era with his studied nonchalance is none other than Eric Menke, Mr. Wentzel's longtime friend.

## COLOPHON

Book design by Donna Sicklesmith Anderson. Typographic consultation by John Michael.
The text for this book has been set in Centaur, which was designed by Bruce Rogers in 1914 for the
Metropolitan Museum of Art, modeled after a type design of Nicolas Jenson's dating from 1470.
The italic is Arrighi, designed by Frederic Warde in 1925 in the style of Italian humanistic
handwriting of 1500. The headlines have been set in Torino, a Bodoni-inspired adaptation.
The printing for this book was performed by Stephenson Printing, a Washington, D.C.
printing company founded in 1959 by George W. Stephenson. The images in this book are tritones
originating from silver-gelatin prints made by Volkmar Kurt Wentzel. Each tritone was
individually separated by Stephenson Printing on a digitized laser scanner in order to capture
the subtle characteristics intended by Mr. Wentzel.

Page 6
*The photograph on this page depicts a medal given to Mr. Wentzel's father.*
*The muse of photography stands in the center with her aides*
*Art on the left and Technology on the right.*
*This medal is a prestigious award for outstanding technical achievement in*
*photography given by the Photographic Society of Vienna, Austria.*
*This society was founded in 1861 and is the oldest in the German speaking countries.*

Page 94
*Mr. Wentzel's mid-1930s view of Washington D.C. looking from Potomac Park*
*toward the city's monumental core.*